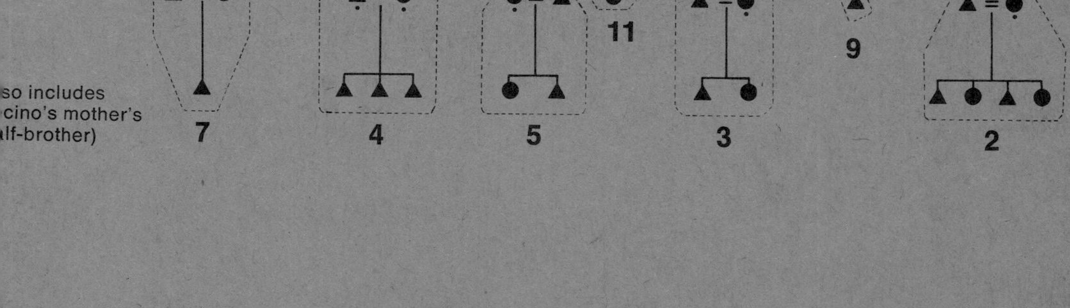
II
I
II
13
11
9
7
4
5
3
2
so includes
cino's mother's
lf-brother)

# NEIGHBORS

Susan Tax Freeman

The University of Chicago Press
Chicago and London

# NEIGHBORS

## The Social Contract in a Castilian Hamlet

International Standard Book Number: 0-226-26169-2
Library of Congress Catalog Card Number: 70-125548
The University of Chciago Press, Chicago 60637
The University of Chicago Press, Ltd., London

Published 1970
Printed in the United States of America

*al Común de Vecinos*

# Contents

# Illustrations

# Tables

# Preface

The study of so small a village as Valdemora has certain advantages for an understanding of Spanish culture, although Valdemora is no more representative of Spain, or even of Old Castile, than is any other single village. I have at least once been taken to task for studying "too small a village," and in this respect I must express my conviction that Valdemora is no less representative of the national spectrum than is any other single village. In a country where regionalism is very pronounced, any locality can be made to look unique, and an attempt to strip social structure of its local color begs the question why regionalism is pronounced and, in any case, produces little that is readable. I have attempted here to treat very local phenomena as part of at least a larger regional type without shattering the portrait of Valdemora itself. My intellectual debt in this endeavor is to my colleagues in Iberian ethnology, past and present. Without the works of Spanish ethnographers of the turn of the century, and of Joaquín Costa in particular, it would be impossible to understand the extent to which Valdemora's corporate tradition is part of a very widespread phenomenon. Without the works of contemporary social anthropologists and sociologists, it would be impossible to see that so small a village as Valdemora is not simply an extreme in Spanish culture but is as legitimately a *version* of that culture as any other single version which has been described in the literature. Indeed, if we regard populations of different sizes and contours as versions of something which they have in common, the question of their representativeness is quite irrelevant. It is thanks to the growing range of Spanish studies that we can begin to point to the themes shared in common by the many local versions of Spanish culture and to examine the Portuguese and French border regions (or other parts of Europe) along comparable lines.

Although its small size distinguishes Valdemora in some ways, neither its territorial boundaries nor the number of its inhabitants serves to limit the Valdemoran's universe. I have commented at some points in the text that the small size of the village seems to force its inhabitants into a larger universe. This is true both in the noncorporate aspects of the social structure described in chapter 5 and in the less tangible value orientation of the villagers, part of which is explored in the final chapter. In the latter respect, Valdemorans are almost city people rather than villagers, and the village is far less isolated socially than are some larger rural settlements which are more diversified internally. But the chief lesson inherent in the case is that the size of a settlement is secondary to the fact that its inhabitants are concentrated in a single place: hamlet, village, town, or city are less important distinctions in Spain than the one between nucleated and dispersed settlement patterns. This, by the way, exemplifies one of the emphases in Spanish culture that is shared by all of the Spanish communities which anthropologists have described and all with which I am passingly familiar, though the local variations of the theme differ and authors may pay more or less attention to them. Therefore, when I say that Valdemorans are part of a universe larger than their own village, I am not only referring to the fact that both their social relationships and their personal ambitions extend beyond the village; I am also saying that their values, cognitive categories, and general style are shared with neighboring settlements, both large and small, and may be studied in a community of any size throughout the region.

Much of this study examines what appear to be very distinct contexts in behavior and behavioral norms in Valdemora. The clarity with which these are observable is due largely to the small size of the village. Similarly, aspects of Valdemora's territorial and religious organization and of the exercise of social control there are accentuated versions of phenomena which seem to be present, but less striking, in larger villages, including those in the immediate vicinity. The clarity of these features in Valdemora is offset by the extent to which other important aspects of Spanish culture are obscured—chiefly, the hierarchic social organization and social stratification, which are again, however, notable in the larger towns in the immediate vicinity. A glance at Valdemora's larger neighbors and a well-posed question to any villager will indicate that the Valdemoran is quite aware that he is part of a larger system. The larger system cannot be studied within the limits of the village. On the other hand, the features of non-hierarchic, horizontal organization within the village are also important in most of Spain, within age groups, occupational groups, or neighborhoods, for example. I feel that some contemporary authors have failed to examine Spanish egalitarian traditions closely enough, partly because they worked in centers where hierarchic traditions claimed their attention first. Here, then, is a Castilian hamlet where taking turns—or "alternating," as it is called—is the order of the day, and where differences in class and wealth do not separate one family from another, where patronage plays no part in villagers' relations with each other, and relations between families are modeled on the ideal of relations between siblings. This, too, is Spain.

The egalitarian tradition so strongly formalized in Valdemora's corporate organization (to be discussed in chapter 2) and reinforced by ceremonial and strong social sanctions (chapter 4) is not a limited, regional phenomenon. Rather, it is a tradition which characterizes interaction in many kinds of groups all over Spain, in populations of all sizes. In this sense, Valdemora simply presents us with a particularly formalized, corporate version of a widespread phenomenon: the expression of common bonds is often ramified by shared ceremonial or common feasting, and people's obligations within a group are ordered on a nonhierarchic basis. On the other hand, it is not overly common that entire communities function on this basis, and in this sense Valdemora serves as a prototype.

Communities resembling Valdemora were documented in Spain around the beginning of the twentieth century, primarily by Joaquín Costa and his colleagues. They found villages of this sort over much of the north of the Iberian peninsula, chiefly in regions of small population centers.[1] They treated each case—and each only briefly—as a unique conglomerate of customs and tended to neglect the general similarities which make of these communities a single type. More recent work in Spain has concentrated on other types—on larger populations. So it is that Valdemora is the first Spanish village of its type to be described at length. For this reason, I will dwell at length, in chapters 2 and 4, on the details of corporate organization. Later chapters will indicate the rapidity with which such things disappear, as they already have in many parts of Europe. Companions to some parts of this study are best sought in the works of historians—above all, in the institutional studies of medieval Europe.

I have included comparative references in the notes and tried to leave the text uncluttered for the general reader. The notes are of necessity suggestive rather than exhaustive, but I have tried to indicate major dimensions—geographic and bibliographic—on which fruitful comparison can be based.

Most of the data presented in the study were gathered in 1963, during my most extended field work in Valdemora. All references

1. I suggest elsewhere (Freeman 1968a) that this distribution may result partly from the intellectual focus of the early writers: they seem to have investigated the south of the peninsula less thoroughly than the north.

to "the present" are from that period, except where I have explicitly incorporated data from 1966 and 1967, especially in the last two chapters.

The names of all of the villages in the Sierra Ministra, except for the centers of Medinaceli and Sigüenza, have been changed, as have the names of Valdemora families. I have protected their identities as well as possible in view of the village's small size. Valdemorans would not like this book, for in my concern with social control I have necessarily dwelt upon the areas of potential rupture between individuals and families. Valdemorans are so concerned with peaceable coexistence that the open discussion of this subject, rather than its minimization, would be quite repugnant to them. I respect their stance, one which succeeds in keeping them at peace, and I apologize for violating their code.

I went to live in Valdemora in 1963 after I had met many of its people during a brief residence in Medinaceli in 1962. I liked and admired them, although I did not yet know why. When I arrived there, I commented on my warm reception in all the houses. I was told, in effect, not to jump to conclusions: "Unfortunately, we're not as nice when we're asked for charity by people who have nothing." One thing, then, that I admired was the honesty of their self-appraisal and their directness—a directness which I never once found to be without grace.

I left Valdemora at the end of 1963. I returned for three months in the summer of 1966 and again in the winter of 1967.

The long documented history of the village, preserved in two parish churches and in an archive in a trunk which passes from house to house with the office of *alcalde*, is richest in data on the nineteenth century, but some aspects of tradition are illuminated by much earlier sources also, beginning around the year 1500. These place in perspective the changes which I have been able to witness in more than five years' acquaintance with Valdemora. I owe much of my understanding of the local archives to the villagers themselves, who read and studied them with me and whose commentaries gave the material its most important dimension. Whatever depth this study may achieve is due to the acute vision of its subjects.

For their help in aspects of my research I would like to thank Julio Caro Baroja and Julio González González. My mother's aid at every stage of the work, beginning with her review of field notes, was especially important for the perspectives she brings from her own years of field experience. The Wenner-Gren Foundation for Anthropological Research supported my work in 1966. My personal debt to its late director, Dr. Paul Fejos, is much older. Marion Sirefman is responsible for much of the production of this book and for drafting the maps and charts. The production was supported by National Institute of Mental Health grant MH 14171-01. I cannot measure my debt to Julian Pitt-Rivers's scholarship and friendship. His Andalusian study presages most of my own offering and, though I assiduously avoided rereading his book while writing mine, I feel that his insights haunt these pages. I am in further debt to two of my most respected colleagues and critics —my father and my husband.

# NEIGHBORS

# 1 The Sierra Ministra

Valdemora has a lot of history.
They say this is the oldest pueblo
in Spain.

—Valdemorans

The Sierra Ministra is part of the great cordillera which forms the southern margin of the Spanish meseta (see map 1). The Sierra marks the three-way divide between the Tajo drainage on the plains to the southwest; the Duero drainage on the high plains of the meseta itself, to the northwest; and the Ebro drainage to the northeast. Some of the major tributaries of these three rivers are born in the Sierra Ministra.

The Sierra is one of the highest inhabited regions of the peninsula. Valdemora is situated at 1107 meters above sea level. Villages at these altitudes are generally small, scattered over the broken terrain along the valleys where tillage is best. Only one town in the region has a present population which exceeds 2000—that is the cathedral city of Sigüenza at the foot of the Sierra (1960 pop. 4715).[1] The region is one of near subsistence-level dry farming of cereal grains and sheepherding. The mountainous terrain has militated against the wide-scale mechanization of agriculture, which has made better progress in the riverine plains to the north and south. The relative scarcity of surface water favors only small-scale irrigation in very limited areas and sharply

1. Instituto Nacional de Estadística 1960.

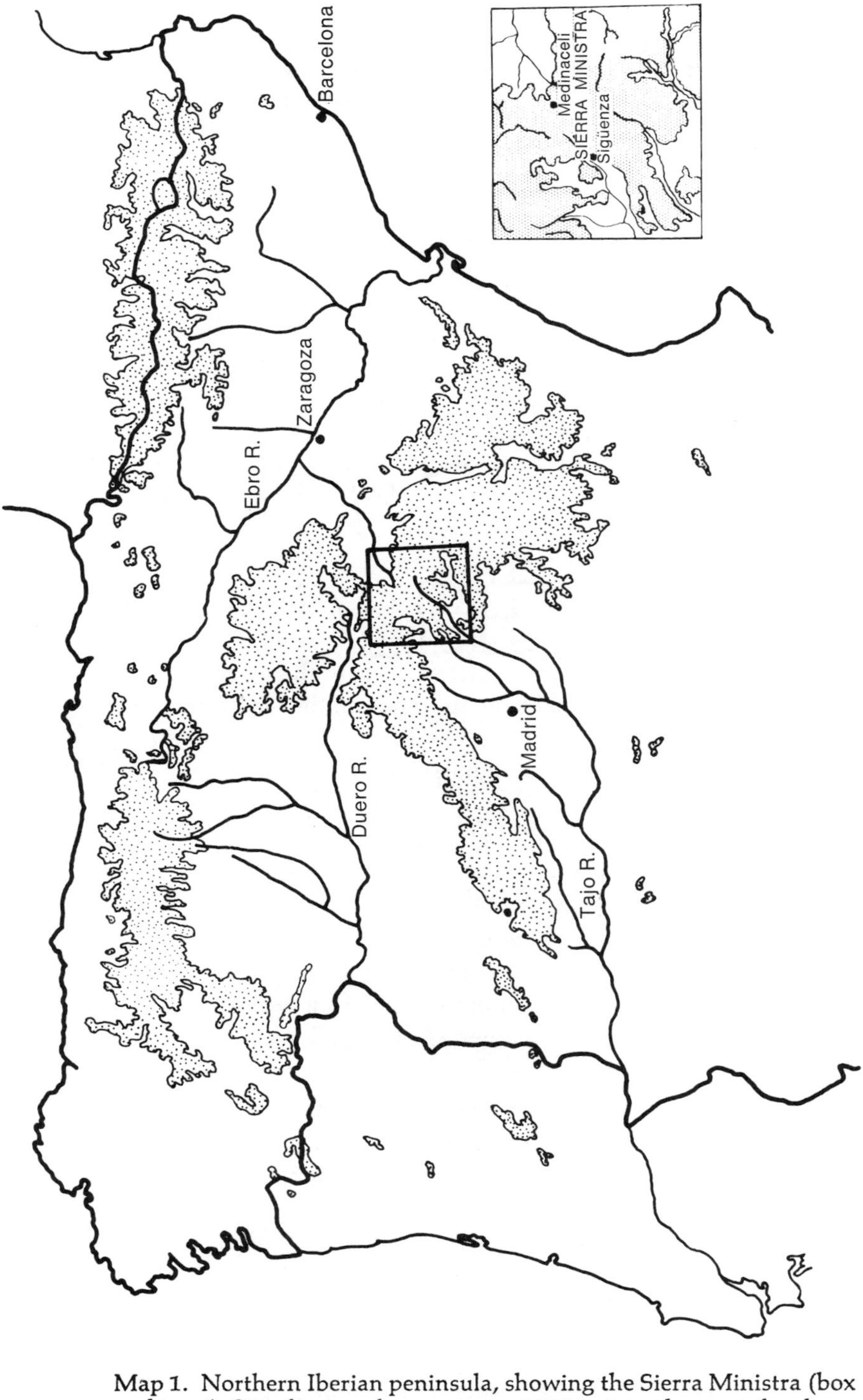


Map 1. Northern Iberian peninsula, showing the Sierra Ministra (box and inset). Stippling marks areas over 1000 meters above sea level. (Adapted from Nuevo atlas de España 1961, p. 175.)

distinguishes the region from the better-watered garden and orchard country of Aragón, immediately to the east. Farmers own most of their own land, or rent some holdings on long-term leases, and are able to produce amply for their families' support. But the possibilities of extensive market production are severely limited by the nature of the terrain, the techniques in use, and, most of all, by the small size of farm holdings. Nor is the area developed industrially in any way. Thus, the individual who wishes to make a better living does so by making a different kind of living, by leaving farming and the Sierra villages altogether and emigrating to a salaried job in some other part of the country. The families who remain in the villages are united by their common way of life. The Sierra Ministra villages are thus marked by the similar nature of their farm economies, by the relative absence of other means of livelihood, and by the small size of their populations. The absence of social and economic stratification dominates the whole texture of village social life.

Valdemora's houses lie huddled at the foot of a conical hill called *el Castillo* (the Castle), as such hills are frequently named in Spain. The living enjoy the sunnier, southern exposure; the dead are buried around the Castillo on its northern face. Fields and pasture surround the Castillo on all sides. The Castillo stands at a bend in the narrow valley which runs north, toward the next town of Salcedo, on the one hand, and east, toward Aguasalida and the Madrid-Barcelona highway, on the other. Travel to Valdemora's other three immediate neighbors—Calzada, Mazarulleque, and Molinos—involves crossing hills, but none of the neighbor villages is more than one hour's walk away (see map 2). Aguasalida is the seat of government for two of its smaller neighbors, Valdemora and Algarabejo. Three kilometers of gravel road connect Valdemora to Aguasalida. Less than 2 kilometers beyond Aguasalida, the road joins the highway. Madrid lies about 150 kilometers to the southwest, and Zaragoza some 170 kilometers to the northeast. But more accessible by traditional means of travel

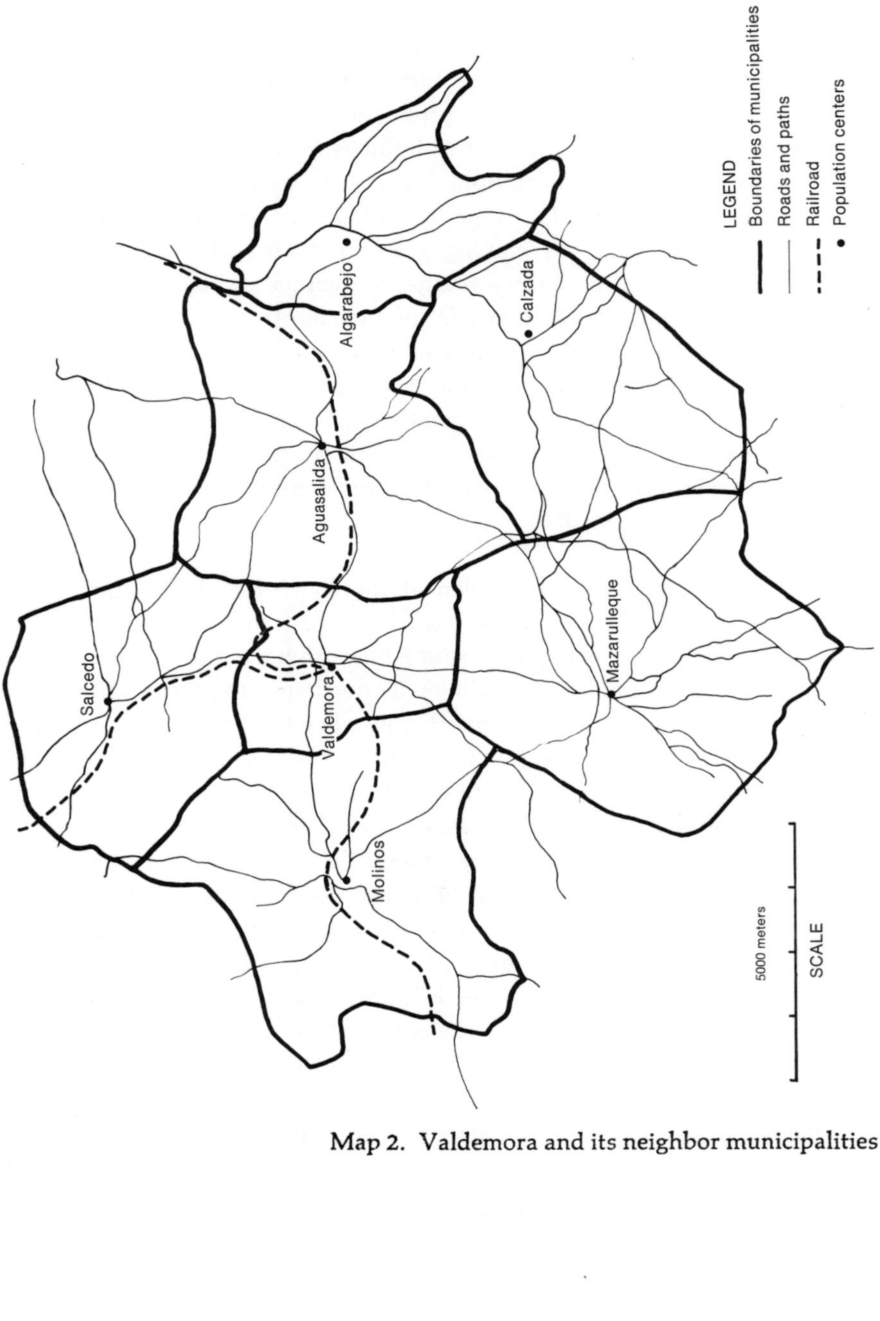


Map 2. Valdemora and its neighbor municipalities

(by foot and mule) are the two historic centers of the region, Medinaceli and Sigüenza, 12 kilometers northeast and 17 kilometers southwest of Valdemora, respectively.

Medinaceli and Sigüenza have been the political and economic focuses of the Sierra Ministra for centuries. The Sierra Ministra itself may be roughly defined as a massif oriented northwest-southeast between the two centers. Although the Sierra today is crossed by the provincial boundary between Guadalajara (in the traditional region of New Castile) and Soria (Old Castile), the boundary has little historical depth. Sigüenza (Guadalajara), the seat of a bishopric, traditionally held ecclesiastical sway over the entire region, whereas secular power lodged in Medinaceli (Soria) and extended over much of the same area. The establishment of provinces in 1833, and the corresponding revision of ecclesiastical provinces, cut Medinaceli's domain in two and assigned those villages in Soria to the bishopric of Osma.

Segontia (Sigüenza) and Ocilis (Medinaceli) were both Celtiberian settlements at the time of the Roman invasion.[2] Ocilis was taken by Roman forces in 153 B.C. High on a hill dominating the valley of the Jalón (a tributary of the Ebro), Ocilis was walled and became a frontier outpost of some importance. The Roman road from Mérida to Caesaraugusta (Zaragoza)—one of the two great throughways—passed Segontia and Ocilis, crossing the present municipalities of Valdemora and Calzada. The great triple arch of Roman construction still stands at the entry of Medinaceli, flanked by the remains of the town's walls; the ruins of the side road which entered the town are still partially visible. Segontia, which had been a Celtiberian military center, became the seat of a bishopric in the sixth century, during the Visigoth domination of Spain, but its ecclesiastical rule was cut short by the Islamic conquest of the peninsula. Ocilis fell to Islamic rule in A.D. 712, the year following the first Muslim conquests on the peninsula, and

2. The early history of the region is summarized in Layna Serrano (1948, 1960), Minguella (1910), and Taracena and Tudela (1962).

Sigüenza is thought to have been entered in 713. Thus began a four-century lapse in Sigüenza's rule and Ocilis' growth into a military center.

Ocilis was renamed Medinaceli (possibly from the Arabic *medinat* [city] + Ocilis, or perhaps from *medinat* + Salim, the name of a supposed founder of the place). In 946 the caliphate at Córdoba decided to make Medinaceli its general army headquarters for what was called the "Central Frontier" or *marca mediana,* replacing Toledo, which now lay too far from the field of operations. Accordingly, Galib al-Nasiri was sent in that year to restore and build up the town, and from that time Medinaceli became a center of Muslim resistance against the reconquest which pushed upon it from the Christian refuge areas in the north. The Arab military leader Almanzor conducted much of his northern campaign from Medinaceli and died there in 1002. The town was also an occasional headquarters of the Cid, Ruy Díaz de Vivar, until his death at Valencia in 1099.[3] The fortified town was a major bone of contention in the definitive Christian reconquest of Castile. It was first reconquered by Alvar Fañez de Minaya in 1104, then recaptured by Muslim forces, and not definitively taken until 1123, by Alfonso I *("el Batallador")* of Aragón and Navarra. At the death of Alfonso I, the territory passed into the possession of Alfonso VII *("el Emperador")* of Castile and León. Before the final conquest of Medinaceli, Sigüenza had been reduced to a mere *aldea,* or dependent hamlet, of Medinaceli. At the time of the capture of Medinaceli, a bishop reentered Sigüenza, and Christian hegemony was reestablished in the Sierra Ministra.[4]

It is impossible to draw a detailed picture of the region under Muslim rule. The Muslim historians of the time were little concerned with demography, and there seem to be no chronicles which might yield data on the composition of the population, par-

3. Some scholars attribute the authorship of the epic poem, *El cantar del mio Cid,* to a native of Medinaceli. Medinaceli is the focal point of the most detailed geographic references contained in the poem. Cf. Reyes 1960.

4. Minguella (1910) dates this event in 1124.

ticularly in frontier regions.[5] It is clear, however, that the Medinaceli frontier was not thickly settled at the time of the Muslim conquest. The foreign population around Medinaceli was probably confined largely to the military installation in the town itself. Muslim population probably did not settle into the countryside to any great extent. Mixing at all levels was much greater in Mediterranean Spain—in the rich agricultural areas of the south and east. Spaniards of such cities as Valencia and Córdoba had far greater contact with Islam in their daily affairs. There is little doubt that the montane, land-bound frontier of Castile was marginal in this respect and did not experience the intensive informal interchange which occurred between the two populations in the south and east. But Muslim administration left its mark on the systems of taxation, military organization, and local officialdom, among others, and in the renaming of many towns and other landmarks.

A period of both informal and planned repopulation of Castile (and the greater part of the peninsula) followed its reconquest. The expulsion of the Muslim populace from the areas of their densest settlement created tremendous gaps in the agricultural countryside as well as in the local capitals. Christian population flowed out of the congested northern refuge area to establish a new balance farther south. New areas were entered under royal *fueros* (grants delimiting areas and conditions of jurisdiction). The Sierra Ministra was probably subject to much more localized population movements. González, the leading historian of the Castilian repopulation, sees the settlement of that whole region less as a reclamation of previously held lands than as a developmental expansion into countryside which had been sparsely settled.[6] Evidence suggests that this expansion involved, for the most part, Castilians from the same general region. The repopulation of Medinaceli itself appears to have been ordered by Alfonso I of Aragón as early as 1104, immediately following the temporary reconquest of the town. The Medinaceli repopulation was ap-

5. Lévi-Provençal 1957, pp. 93–94.
6. González 1951, 1960.

parently used as a model for further repopulation in Aragón. The Medinaceli fuero included within its boundaries the dependency of Sigüenza and extended to the river Tajo on the south. Upon his accession to these domains, Alfonso VII of Castile and León ordered the special repopulation of Sigüenza. The episcopal see was reestablished there, but Sigüenza remained under the civil jurisdiction of Medinaceli. Soon Sigüenza was granted greater autonomy. In 1138 Alfonso VII granted to Sigüenza settlement rights for one hundred married men and their families, of which only twenty could be from Medinaceli. The cathedral and population center referred to were located in "Lower" Sigüenza. "Upper" Sigüenza was a separate nucleus centering on a castle and two churches. In 1146 Alfonso granted to the bishop of Sigüenza jurisdiction over Upper as well as Lower Sigüenza. Thus, Sigüenza became a cathedral city with a unified town council, recognizing no lord other than the bishop.[7] But its ties with Medinaceli were hardly severed, as becomes evident in the feudal history of the region.

The period of the reconquest yields better data on the composition of the population than are available from earlier dates.[8] The greater part of the Muslim minority was to be found, as expectable, farther south, especially in Toledo, in countryside and city, as both freemen and slaves. But small neighborhoods of *Mudéjares* (Muslims under Christian domain) were to be found in northern cities as well, and some Castilian fueros were granted specifically to them. The Mudéjares were eventually forced to become baptized, were called *Moriscos*, and were finally expelled from Spain in 1609. Some *Mozárabes* (Christians from Muslim domains) resided in Medinaceli.

A large Jewish population was long established in Spain by

7. González 1960, 1:101, 453.

8. Among the studies of minority groups in medieval Spain are Amador de los Ríos (1960), Caro Baroja (1961), Castro (1954), de las Cagigas (1947), González (1960).

the time of the Muslim conquest. The Jews were almost exclusively urban and largely commercial in calling, handling the bulk of the nation's commerce, their services heavily depended upon by the Crown. After the reconquest of Castile, Jews from farther south migrated into Castile in flight from persecution under the Muslim *taifas* (small kingdoms formed after the fall of the caliphate). These refugees swelled the Jewish quarters of the towns and doubtless brought in foreign ways from al-Andalus, the heavily Islamic realm. Sigüenza and Medinaceli, like most other towns in Spain, had sizeable Jewish populations.[9] Rabal notes that Soria's three-hundred-house *aljama* (Jewish sector) overflowed onto the Plaza Mayor and that there was a second aljama in another part of town.[10] Medinaceli had one of the larger Jewish populations in the region. The Medinaceli aljama and that of Sigüenza were taxed as a unit as residents of the bishopric. Each aljama had a synagogue, of course. Some of these were converted into Roman Catholic churches, some were sold, and some fell into ruin when the Jews were expelled from Spain in 1492. The present Jeronymite convent of Medinaceli was probably at one time a synagogue. Documents record the purchase of the synagogue of Sigüenza, by a doctor of that town, for twenty thousand *maravedis* on 19 December 1496.[11]

On the basis of tax lists drawn up at the end of the thirteenth century, Amador de los Ríos estimates the number of taxpaying Jews in Castilian domains to have been 854,951.[12] (The region includes at least parts of modern New Castile.) Taxpayers were males only, either twenty years of age or, if younger, already married. The actual population would have approached thrice the number of taxpayers. These figures seem high, but data on the dimensions of the Jewish emigration and conversion at the time

9. Cf. Amador de los Ríos 1960.
10. Rabal 1889, pp. 183–84.
11. Cantera Burgos 1955.
12. Amador de los Ríos 1960, pp. 298–302.

of the expulsion support the assumption that Spain's Jewish population was perhaps as large as that.[13]

Finally, a feature of the new Christian kingdom of Castile was the presence in most of its capital cities of resident foreigners—both non-Castilians and natives of other European countries. During the Muslim rule, the growth of the shrine of Saint James the Apostle at Santiago de Compostela (Galicia) into Europe's most important pilgrimage center brought a steady flow of foreigners and new influences across the narrow northern belt of Christian territory into Spain's far northwest corner. The *Camino de Santiago* (Road to Santiago) was more than just a pilgrimage route; it effectively linked northern Spain with the rest of Europe at a time when most of the peninsula was severed and shielded from such contacts. The Camino became an international throughway which served as a route of entry for a variety of commercial and cultural influences. A number of Christian religious orders (most notably the Cluniac order) were first established in Spain at this time. Américo Castro draws from *Las crónicas anónimas de Sahagún* a picture of the cosmopolitan settlements which developed along the Camino:

> Around the abbeys, towns grew up composed of people from everywhere, attracted by the wealth of the road to Santiago: Gascons, Bretons, Germans, Englishmen, Burgundians, Normans, Tolosans, Provençals, Lombards, and many other tradesmen of divers nations and foreign tongues.[14]

After the reconquest, enclaves of foreigners, usually with special civil status, persisted in many Castilian and Aragonese capitals, particularly along the Camino. González, writing of the reign of Alfonso VIII (1158–1214), regards the foreign colony at Burgos as the most important one of the period. Its greatest numbers were French, among the Catalan, English, German, and Italian residents.

A full ethnohistory of the Castilian frontier, if sources for it

13. Cf. Roth 1947.
14. Castro 1954, p. 180.

exist, has not been produced. But available sources indicate that the region was truly a Marca Mediana, lying between the Spain of Santiago and the Spain of the Muslim conquest, exposed to some of the influences of both and, perhaps, escaping some of their pressures. The frontier capitals shared some if not all of the heterogeneity of their larger neighbors, whereas the farm population was probably dominantly Castilian. The documents of the feudal period finally begin to reveal the character of the countryside, with elements which continue to distinguish it at present.

Medinaceli was the small, cosmopolitan seat of a frontier fuero when, in 1370, it became the seat of the County of Medinaceli. In that year the King of Castile, Enrique II, conferred the title of Count of Medinaceli on Bernal de Bearn, a bastard son of the Count of Foix. In 1479 the Catholic Kings, Ferdinand and Isabela, raised the title of the fifth count to that of duke. The boundaries of the Duchy appear to have coincided essentially with those of the original fuero, though the ties with Sigüenza were now of a different nature. The entire Sierra Ministra is referred to in documents of the time as the Sierra *del Ducado* (of the Duchy) Valdemora was equally called *del Castillo* and *del Ducado*. *Del Ducado* is still part of the official name of many villages in the region, and many others are officially *de Medinaceli*. The House of Medinaceli was at first supported by a royal salt grant, proceeding from the salt deposits below the town at Salinas de Medinaceli. Rights to some of the salt had already been granted in the thirteenth century and perhaps at other times as well.[15] By the sixteenth century, the salt grant provided insufficient support for the ducal house, and permission was obtained for the establishment in Medinaceli of a collegiate church. The secular power thereby gained rights to some of the revenue accruing to the Church establishment in its domain. The fortunes of the Duchy at this period cannot be considered apart from the contemporary events attending the expulsion of the Jewish population from Spain. The loss

15. González 1960, 3:311, 613.

in revenue from the high taxes which had been levied on the Jews, in addition to the loss of the realm's most important commercial and financial personnel, had profound effects on the local as well as the national economy. The lists of recipients of the tributes levied on the aljamas of Castile speak eloquently for the fact that the Jews were prime sources of support of the local nobility.[16] It is probably no coincidence that from this epoch, from the final years of the fifteenth century, are dated the first known transactions of the Duchy with the individual villages under its domain with respect to the acquisition of ducal rights to village common lands.[17]

The towns of the Sierra Ministra were organized into groups called *cuadrillas,* which were features of the pastoral organization predating the feudal regime (see chapter 2). These town-leagues apparently dealt as units with the Duchy, for some purposes at least, and the ducal archives are indexed by cuadrillas. Valdemora was one of seventeen towns belonging to the cuadrilla of Calzada, its neighbor village.[18] Calzada was the first of this group to record an agreement (dated 1499) giving the Duchy rights to tax the produce of the pasture and woodland of the village. Valdemora's accord with the Duchy is dated 1539 but contains reference to negotiations on the matter as early as 1504. The agreement provides for the payment by the village of certain fees proportional

16. Amador de los Ríos 1960, pp. 916–31.

17. The documents preserved in the ducal archives, in Seville, probably contain sufficient material for a detailed institutional and economic history of the Duchy, although they have never been fully utilized. Paz y Melia (1922) traces the macro-history of the Duchy and does not deal with its organization. Fernández de Béthencourt (1904) provides primarily genealogical and heraldic history. The emphasis upon preservation of the more spectacular materials only has already resulted (ca. 1960) in the destruction of carloads of village tax records and miscellany as "waste paper." Remains of this "waste" heap indicate that a patient historian might have found there the raw material for a major demographic, economic, and institutional study of Castilian feudal organization.

18. Documents concerning this cuadrilla are filed in the ducal archives in the Casa de Pilatos, Seville, under the Medinaceli title, *legajo* 48. See Appendix, sec. 1.

to the amounts of wood cut from the communal woodlands and of the grass and leaves collected from the woods, pasture, and meadow of the village domain. The Duchy acquired such rights in all of the villages in its jurisdiction, which numbered ninety-six in 1594.[19] Three-fourths of the amount Valdemora paid the Duchy was to be returned to the council of Valdemora and one-fourth went to the presiding judge of the tribunal, evidently a ducal employee. The council was probably responsible for turning over all or most of its share to the Duchy; the system persists today with the annual payment of a given sum by the town council to the House of Medinaceli.

The rights of the Duchy to the produce of woodland and pasture, with the produce of the salt mines, appear to be the only ones which the secular lord maintained independent of Church rights in the area. In all other cases, the lord received revenues by special arrangement with the regional ecclesiastical powers, who allowed portions of Church income to be diverted in support of the lord, probably in exchange for a variety of services. Such arrangements differed from one locality in Spain to another. Both the ducal and village archives are silent on the details of Valdemora's relations with the Duchy and with Sigüenza for the two centuries following the agreement with the Duchy in 1539, though the ducal archives preserve some reports rendered to the Duke by the cuadrilla concerning its use of the pastures. The Cadaster of the Marqués de la Ensenada, recorded around 1750, yields a full description of the way in which tributes were channeled to the regional centers of power.[20] Throughout the realm, it was the Church which levied general taxes. The *diezmo*, or tithe, was an annual assessment of one-tenth of the grain harvest and of all

19. Jimeno 1958.

20. This survey, for purposes of tax assessment, was instituted under the regime of the Marqués de la Ensenada as minister of Hacienda, beginning in 1748. Most of the nation was surveyed and the data on many regions are still preserved. García-Badell (1963, pp. 241–46) gives a history of the survey. The Valdemora cadaster is preserved both in the Hacienda archive for the province and in the Valdemora town archive.

other produce, including one-tenth of the livestock born during the year. The *primicia*, or assessment of first fruits, was a fixed tax of one-half *fanega* of wheat or barley for every yield of ten and one-half fanegas or more.[21] The Valdemora town council assessed each of its members for the amounts he owed and divided the collected total in the following way. The local parish priest received the entire first fruits of wheat and barley, and all of the "minor" tithes (on suckling pigs, chickens, honey, wax, and young mules, asses, and bovids). Of the "major" tithes (wheat and barley), one-fifteenth went to "various interested parties" of whose identity we know nothing more. The remainder was divided into three parts, one for the bishop and church of Sigüenza, one for the parish priest, and one to be divided between the collegiate church of Medinaceli and the Duke of Medinaceli. The wool tithe was distributed in the same way. Of the tithe of oats, one-fifteenth was subtracted as above, and the remainder was divided between the parish priest and Sigüenza.

In addition to exacting tithes from villagers, the Church held title to a great deal of village land, much of it in mortmain, on which farmers had to pay rent. Church property in 1750 totalled almost 97 hectares, about three times the amount owned by farmers themselves (see table 1). Almost all of the Church holdings were farmed for the standard rental rate of one fanega of wheat and/or barley (the bread grains of the time) per fanega of land.[22] The average farmer was paying rent on more than half of the land he worked and also paying tithes and first fruits and contributing his part to the rental of ducal pasture and other communal fees. Cadastral materials from 1879 vividly illustrate the shifts in ownership which occurred after the disamortization and public sale of Church lands in 1837: Church holdings in Valde-

21. The fanega of volume is the amount of grain required to sow one fanega (surface) of land. The Castilian fanega of land is 2236 square meters. The fanega of wheat is 43.5 kg., of barley 37.0 kg., and of oats 27.0 kg.

22. The modern bread grain is wheat only. The customary rate for land rental today is one fanega of wheat per fanega of land.

TABLE 1

Land Ownership in Valdemora as Recorded in Cadasters (in hectares)

| | Owners | | | | |
|---|---|---|---|---|---|
| | Vecinos[a] | Outsiders[b] | Church | Council | Duchy |
| 1750 | 31.6514 | 3.7271 | 96.8829 | 308.0275 | 316.9725 |
| 1879 | 47.5709 | 64.5093 | 3.9770 | 308.0275[c] | 316.9725[c] |
| 1935–63[d] | 87.6094 | 38.7023 | 0.0000 | 17.3005 | 429.8630 |

NOTE: Only the 1935 cadaster is based on precise land survey. No general maps accompany the earlier surveys. Rather, the 1750 and 1879 documents list the sizes and the locations of different fields by owners.

[a] The difference between the three years is apparently greater than is shown here: although the documents for 1750 and 1879 appear to include under a farmer's name all of the land he worked for his nonfarmer siblings, the 1935–63 figures here show only the individual holdings and not those of the siblings. Thus, the size of the consolidated family estates in 1963 would contrast even more sharply if we considered them in their entirety.

[b] Excluding the Duchy and the relatives of vecinos.

[c] The 1879 cadaster gives no figure for ducal or council holdings, but they seem to have been approximately the same as in 1750. The 1935 figure for ducal holdings is larger than earlier ones, because vecinos say that they allowed some unused, low-quality fields to be surveyed as ducal pasture in 1935. Many of these, apparently, were formerly owned by the council.

[d] Entries in this row total lower than the other two rows because emigrant-siblings' holdings and railroad lands have been excluded.

mora were reduced to a mere 4 hectares by 1879. Historians have deplored the disamortization legislation on the grounds that the ensuing sale of Church lands gave entry into the villages to well-to-do outsiders, who bought up lands and continued to extract rents just as the Church had done. In this sense it is true that the disamortization was hardly a reform. Cadastral data from Valdemora indicate the large-scale purchase of former Church lands primarily by a single man, Mariano Benito, who never lived in Valdemora; his lands were held in rent by Valdemora farmers. But the 1837 legislation also abolished the Church's right to collect tithes and first fruits. As we read between the lines of cadastral history, it was the farmer's freedom from the burden of these taxes which marked the turning-point in the village economy. At last, the farmer was able to accumulate some surplus. By 1935 all of Mariano Benito's holdings had been purchased by farmers of the village. The amount of land in the municipality held by the farmers themselves increased from 31.65 hectares in 1750 to 47.57 hectares in 1879. Today's figure stands at 87.61 hectares. The outsiders who today hold land in Valdemora are mostly farmers from the neighboring villages who acquire them through marriage or inheritance, and Valdemorans have similar holdings in the other villages.

The abolition of Church taxes on peasant produce broke the back of the feudal regime which had depended upon tithes for its major support. The House of Medinaceli was left with only its original rights in the villages—rights to certain rents on common pasture and woodland. These rights are still preserved today in many of the Sierra villages. Valdemora still pays a fixed annual rent to the Duchy, now housed in Seville. Some villages have bought their lands from the Duchy; in others, groups of farmers rather than the village corporations have made the purchase. For towns like Valdemora, in which ducal tenure continues, the Duchy maintains a part-time administrator in Medinaceli. The federal taxes which the Duchy must pay on Valdemora's lands, plus the expenses of administration, exceed by far the amount of the rent paid by the village.

The once thriving *villa* of Medinaceli has lost two-thirds of its population since 1849.[23] No longer are markets and livestock fairs held there, nor do villagers travel there to do business with the lord. It is no longer a home of nobles: the palaces are closed, the coats of arms above their doors eroded. The ducal palace, shuttered and cool, is sometimes used for the storage of apples en route to Madrid from the orchards of Aragón. The Civil Guard for the area has headquarters in the town, perhaps because there are so many empty buildings for its use; their wives complain of the hard conditions, since the closest source of water is located outside the walls and down the hillside. Taracena and Tudela, the provincial historians of Soria, give a regretful analysis of Medinaceli's decline:

23. Madoz 1849; Instituto Nacional de Estadística 1960.

> The very valley to which she owed her importance is now ridding her of it. If a road, the Royal Road, once instilled vitality there, other roads, the railroad and the highway, are absorbing the life out of her, and into the Jalón valley and to the station at Salinas is flowing what little is left of the villa's life; the scanty population of the villa is being reduced drop by drop, inhabitant by inhabitant, and even house by house, for roofs, doors, and windows are falling in.[24]

The National Office of Fine Arts, however, has not overlooked Medinaceli's role in the kaleidoscope of Spain's history: her recent designation as a national monument insures Medinaceli's survival in the Age of Tourism.

Sigüenza, on the other hand, stands in the valley through which the rail lines pass and has been able to keep pace with the times. It is the commercial *chef lieu* of the Sierra Ministra. Traveling by rail, the Sierra villagers visit Sigüenza with much greater frequency than ever before.

The Madrid-Zaragoza-Barcelona rail lines were laid in the 1870s. Valdemora is the village nearest the junction where a branch line joins the east-west lines. Towns along both routes have had some small settlement of outsiders, who are employed by the railroad or postal service. There has been a railroad population in Valdemora ever since 1870. A period of very heavy construction, when new lines were laid, occurred from 1948 to about 1951. Most of the work force was transient, with rapid turnover. The permanent railroad settlement is also transient in that none of the families is from Valdemora and few are located there for more than three or four years. In 1963 there were 173 persons living in the railroad development near the station. The junction makes the station a fairly important one which employs a larger work force than other stations. Nevertheless, by 1966 this force was reduced by about half, because many minor jobs became obsolete and ceremonial positions like that of the special guards were abolished. Valdemorans foresee the further diminution of the station's importance with the great increase in Spain's highway traffic.

24. Taracena and Tudela 1962, p. 215 (my translation).

The station barrio, or neighborhood, is located about one-half kilometer below the village, along the curving valley bottom, and the one place cannot be seen from the other. The station settlement and the farm village are always distinguished by the residents as the station barrio and the pueblo, respectively. The former station, on the old tracks, abandoned in 1961, was closer to the pueblo itself, facing the west side of the Castillo from the adjoining part of the valley. The construction of the new tracks and station brought with it recognition of the fact that the tiny pueblo's facilities were inadequate for use by both farmers and railroad workers. Thus, in 1952, the government supported the construction of a new church-school complex located between the pueblo and the site of the future new station.

The presence of a nonfarming population in the vicinity allows Valdemora to support more commercial activity than could the farmers alone. From the construction period starting in 1948 date the activities of a fishmonger from Aguasalida, who receives his fish by train and serves Valdemora, Aguasalida, and Salcedo; two butchers, from Molinos and Mazarulleque, who do their major trade with the salaried railroad workers; and a small general-store keeper from Aguasalida, who divides his time between the two towns. In the same period a commercial bakery began to serve the town's daily needs, selling lesser amounts to several other towns as well, and the farmers' wives gradually began to admit that the baker's bread was as good as their own and ceased their weekly baking in the communal oven of the village. The bar-restaurant of the station has been important in social life, especially that of the men, as long as there has been a station. Aside from all these enterprises, which Valdemora farmers can patronize more regularly than farmers from other towns, the railroad itself serves as a vehicle for supplying wanted goods. Some of its employees have access to produce from their homes in other regions, and they market this in Valdemora. No villager is without connections on the railroad, and anyone can send orders to his favorite Sigüenza business and receive the merchandise by return train, or send messages to any town or capital on the railroad without paying postage. Valdemorans can travel with ease, whereas the residents of surrounding villages must come to the station by foot or by mule. None of the farmers owns a car; a few use bicycles; and the few men who own motor scooters are constantly sought by their friends for transport. People who travel less, for whatever reason, are aided by their more mobile neighbors; in this way, messages and goods are constantly being carried from town to town, from the station to the pueblo, and to more distant villages.

But for all of their contact and sharing of facilities, the village and the station barrio remain separate in many ways. The station people do not share a common tradition with each other or with the villagers, and they have no real commitment to life in Valdemora. They depend upon their salaries rather than upon the land, and it is the land that holds the pueblo together. The context in which the two communities are most sharply separated and those in which there is more interaction will be discussed later.

The small size of Valdemora's population has crucial implications for many aspects of its social structure. The size of the population has been relatively stable for as long as it can be documented. The earliest available records show an early sixteenth-century population of nine farm families. The cadaster for 1750 lists the same number. The 1879 cadaster lists fourteen. The census of 1900 lists fifteen inhabited houses, a number which appears to exceed the number of operating farms in that year.[25] In 1963 there were thirteen households, one with a widowed and one with a retired head, living on the land; one of these households left town in 1965. There is some fluctuation in the number of operating farms from generation to generation, and this process can be traced in detail, but the limits within which these shifts take place are narrow. Ten estates were farmed separately in 1963; there were nine after 1965.

25. A father and his married son who farm a single estate usually occupy separate households.

A close analysis of cadastral data gives evidence of a pattern of tenure which once gave all families equal shares of each different kind of land, though the passing centuries have brought disorder to that pattern. Whether Valdemora was founded in the period of the repopulation, or if it is older, is not known. The closely ordered division of resources and regulation of their use, to be described in chapter 2, are features of village organization so widespread in Europe that it is not possible to assign their presence in one locality to so limited a historical development as the repopulation. But, on the other hand, there is no question that the repopulation movement fostered the foundation of new settlements in conformity with this familiar type. The town's age is not important for the major point which concerns us here: with the traditional techniques in use, the plot of land which *is* Valdemora and whose boundaries have been clearly drawn for at least 450 years could not ever have supported a significantly larger population than the present one. This is true of all of the Sierra villages, whose populations rarely exceed two hundred or, formerly, three hundred. The broken topography itself favors small, rather than large, population centers for the practice of the traditional agriculture of the region. Furthermore, from the time of the earliest reference to these villages, there has been no frontier to support population expansion. The lack of new lands to work and the impossibility of exploiting by traditional means lands outside a certain radius from the center, even if they were available, are facts of life which dwell constantly in the farmers' minds.

Small population size fosters a high rate of intervillage marriage in the Sierra in general, so that the types of marriage which are preferred throughout Spain are not as frequent in the Sierra as elsewhere (see chapter 5). One of the results of such frequent marrying out is that families of a single village are not able to amass property through repeated intermarriage, generation after generation. Marrying out exerts a levelling force on the population: since property means wealth and status, and since property cannot be concentrated in significant amounts for significant lengths of time, there is no real social stratification in the village. This would not be the case if the Sierra offered opportunities for wealth by means other than wheat farming, but it has not been exploited in other ways. The land is relatively poor and produces no luxury items; the area is undeveloped industrially; it is too hot in summer and too cold in winter for the real development of a tourist or vacation trade.

So it is that the Sierra Ministra has been left alone, though it has not in any sense been isolated. Mariano Benito, and some others like him, bought land in Valdemora, but never chose to live there. All of the villages supported the Duchy, but the nobility lived only in Medinaceli and eventually left there as well. It is significant, for example, that none of the large chaplaincies once held in mortmain in Valdemora was donated by a resident farmer of the village; to the farmers, such extravagant gestures were foreign. The traditional village social life is one which is not marked by the co-residence of the rich and the poor, the landowner and his tenant, the noble and the commoner. People who are neighbors in the village are equals in status and treat one another as such. Those who command respect as social superiors are also inevitably outsiders, and this fact allows the Valdemoran to demand respect in return, for the villager is a member of a corporation which ultimately regards the foreigner as an outcast and, if provoked, does not stop short of treating him as such. The collective action which Lope de Vega dramatized in *Fuente Ovejuna* represents a dire extreme, but it is an extreme which has more than once come to life in Spain; the forces from which it grows lie at the heart of the village structure to be examined here.

Valdemora knows no such phenomenon as crystallized political factions. Identical responsibilities of village membership fall equally upon all, and the sanctions of public opinion are exercised relentlessly by every family upon every other. Village cohesion is, if anything, strengthened by the collisions with outside forces which might fragment more heterogeneous populations. The tensions which exploded into the Civil War of 1936, for example, did not find strong partisans of one or another cause in the village.[26] This piece of recent history is illustrative of the fact that it is possible to draw a portrait of Valdemora in those years, and of the war as seen from that village, on which there is community consensus. The community is not divided by differences in wealth, religious sentiment, or access to power which would foster different loyalties and conflicting views of the events of the war. As small property holders, the Sierra farmers in 1936 constituted a relatively satisfied group, uncommitted to revolutionary goals, but also mistrustful of the conservative powers with which it had long familiarity. Religiously, the area is conservative, but only with respect to traditional religious values and not with respect to the maintenance of clerical power. There were no individuals in the villages or branches of any establishments (other than the Church) which were important enough to create vested interests there (and the only person with a vested interest in the Church is the parish priest, who is outnumbered). The single commitment of the villagers was to farming wheat and staying alive, and their experience with all governments was that they were administered from outside and levied taxes. The Sierra Ministra again became a frontier. The Nationalists had general control in the region from the time of their first rising.[27] But the front, during the first months of the war, lay right at Sigüenza. A few younger Valdemoran men left the land to do military service, most of them drafted into Nationalist forces. Their former loyalties are hard to discern today, partly for political reasons, but mostly because the partisan issues were not very much alive for them.

Valdemora set about the business of survival. Villagers look

26. Lisón-Tolosana (1966) is able to trace in detail the different sympathies of divergent interest groups in a highly stratified Aragonese town. This cannot be done for Valdemora. The two towns present polar contrasts in many respects. Lisón-Tolosana was able to build his entire study on the notion of internal stratification, which creates a strong centrifugal force in the town's life, whereas in Valdemora the observer is made constantly aware of centripetal pressures on the unstratified population.

27. Thomas 1961, pp. 162–64.

back upon the war as a senseless interlude growing out of human frailty, a brutal rupture of sane social life which no cause could justify. Their approach was to remain aloof when possible and to yield when necessary. This they did as a community. When troops (of both sides), camped in the Sierra, demanded food, the *alcalde* (mayor) assessed all families for equal amounts and sent food into the hills. This is regarded as the only intelligent thing to have done. Documents indicate that a similar method was employed when troops involved in the Napoleonic War demanded food in 1812: the amount given them was deducted from the holdings of the then-extant communal granary. In 1936, several individuals in the area who refused troops' demands were killed, and Valdemorans regard them as having wasted their lives for want of a little intelligent realism. As the siege of Madrid continued and the front lines moved away from the Sierra (before the war was one year old), acquiescence to the government in power was life's simple rule, as it had been under both the Monarchy and the Republic.

The ties binding villagers—both the formal, corporate ties and those arising from the common way of life—are strong enough that the village is able to assume a unified "personality," surmounting internal differences in many of its dealings with outside forces. This personality emerges again and again, in a variety of contexts, and the forces which underlie it must be explored as central to the understanding of village culture. But if a villager's membership in the corporate body is crucial, so also are all of the respects in which his actions are not bound by such membership. Every Valdemoran has an extended network of kinsmen and friends; his relationships with them are of an order apparently different from those with his neighbors. There is a constant dialectic between the activities of the village qua corporation and the actions of its members as private individuals. The corporate village is closed and finite, but the networks of kinship and acquaintanceship are not. The influences which operate to bring about change are frequently introduced to the corporate village by way of the contact networks of some of its members. With reference to each system, a seemingly different set of imperatives governs people's interactions; even the operative models of kinship change in different social contexts. Thus, the central task of this study is to outline the features of both the communal and the private spheres of action in Valdemora, with the attendant rules governing social behavior, and to observe the way in which the systems interact to form, for the Valdemoran, a single, coherent world.

# 2 The Corporate Village

What's that man doing there—
there in the dark? What's he
doing that nobody's with him,
and what's he thinking or what's
he working at?. . . Not having
anybody with him there, he'll
always be in the dark.

—A Valdemora widow in response
to Murray TAT Card 20

Membership in the village corporation, the *común de vecinos,* is based upon the effective ownership and active farming of a diversified farm within Valdemora's boundaries. The ownership of one or two parcels of land, or even inherited rights to an estate, do not make one a member of the común; one must actively work a diversified estate known as an *heredad.* This term refers specifically to cultivable lands of the different kinds necessary for full subsistence: cereal lands for the bread-grain, wheat; for the fodder-grains, barley and oats; and for legumes; and irrigable plots for the cultivation of vegetables. Although a farmer may generally sell or rent out at will individual parcels of his estate, the disposition of an entire estate may occur only through inheritance or by sale to a known person as authorized by the común. The común thus maintains control over the composition of its membership. This control has never, to anyone's knowledge, had to be exercised by force. When a farmer dies and leaves no heirs who wish to work the land, it is simply understood that other resident farmers have first option to rent the estate or, as a group, to release it to an outsider. In past times, particularly under the feudal regime, outsiders did attain ownership of several estates, as evidenced even in the modern cadaster, but the effective control of these lands remains with the farmers of the village who lease them in perpetuity; rights to farm these estates pass through the inheritance system from a farmer to his children. In most instances, the owners of these lands have never visited the village. Aside from the few owners in this category, the only men not born in the village who own land there also work it; they have indeed acquired rights to it through inheritance and are not total foreigners to Valdemora. One man decided to work the holdings inherited from his mother, though he grew up in his father's village; another was named legal heir by his farmer stepfather, who had no children of his own. A man may also become a member of the común by actively farming his wife's holdings in the village, though it is more common for a woman's brother, rather than her husband, to work the estate.

Común membership is not confined to the active farmer (or the retired farmer) alone, but includes his wife and unmarried children—the same individuals who typically reside together under one roof. A married son, if he works the land, is the head of a separate household which constitutes a separate unit of común membership (thereby placing the father in at least partial retirement). A bachelor farmer cannot enter the común before his father's death, when he attains the title to the estate he works. Details of these arrangements are discussed in the next chapter. Here it is sufficient to say that the común embraces the nuclear families of the farmers and that farm households are its constituent units, whereas the town council *(concejo)* is composed of the male heads of family only. The council is the official voice and the executive body of the común. The council holds frequent business meetings. The común gathers in its entirety only on ritual occasions, but the functions of the council cannot be divorced from the interests of the households that its members represent.

Members of the común are known as *vecinos.* This term has various applications which must be clarified. In the broadest sense, a vecino (neighbor) of a place is simply a legal resident of that place as defined by the civil code. Valdemorans of the pueblo formally distinguish themselves from the vecinos "of civil status" in the railroad population by use of the terms vecinos "of the pueblo" or vecinos "of the común." But in daily usage they simply equate vecinos with farmers, as opposed to *los de la RENFE*[1] (the railroad people) or *los de abajo* (the people down the hill). There is, however, a further distinction made within the pueblo. Traditional usage applies the term *vecino* only to the male heads of farm families—that is, to married men who work the land or, in the case of bachelors, to adult male farmers whose inherited shares of land already stand legally in their names. (As will be elaborated in chapter 3, an heir who farms will acquire usufruct of an estate at the time of his or her marriage, but titles are not transferred until the death of the father and sometimes also the mother, and then all children inherit equal shares.) The traditional status of vecino generates a distinction between members of vecino families as active or retired farm families and people who grew up in vecino families and own title to lands, but do and have not farmed them. The latter are known as *hijos del pueblo* (children of the pueblo) and are recognized in some, but not all, respects as kinsmen and insiders when they reside in the pueblo. In such a position are a number of sons of the pueblo who have maintained local residence and work on the railroad, or daughters of the pueblo who have married nonfarmers in the vicinity. These people all choose to reside in the pueblo rather than near the station. I shall use the word vecino in its traditional sense, in reference to farm families and often specifically to their male heads.

The pueblo population in 1963 and 1966 and details of household composition are summarized in table 2. The status of one family, Household 12, requires comment. The family head is one of a group of siblings who inherited land in Valdemora. Three of his brothers work their shares together, whereas he chose to spend only the time necessary to work his small portion and was other-

1. RENFE designates Red Nacional de Los Ferrocarriles Españoles (Spanish National Railways).

TABLE 2
Pueblo Composition, 1963 and 1966

| 1963 | | | | Changes by 1966 | | | |
|---|---|---|---|---|---|---|---|
| Status of Head and Household Number | Number of Persons in Household | Relation of Household Members to Head | Remarks | Born | Immig. | Emig. | Died |
| Active Vecino | | | | | | | |
| 1 | 4 | W,D,MFS | | | | | |
| 2 | 6 | W,S,S,D,D | | S | | | |
| 3* | 4 | W,S,D | | | | | |
| 4 | 5 | W,S,S,(S)* | | | | | |
| 5 | 4 | W,S,D | | | | D | |
| 6 | 4 | W,D,D | | | | | |
| 7 | 3 | W,S | | | | | |
| 8 | 5 | W,S,S*,S* | Father and son farm together | | | S,S | |
| 9* | 2 | M | Bachelor vecino | | | | |
| 10 | 2 | B | Bachelor vecino and younger brother farm with Household 6, share hearth with Household 14 | | | | |
| Retired Vecino | | | | | | | |
| 11 | 3 | W,D | | | | D | |
| Child of Pueblo | | | | | | | |
| 12* ♂ | 5 | W,S,S,S | Also farms small holding | | | Whole family | |

TABLE 2—*cont.*

| 1963 | | | | Changes by 1966 | | | |
|---|---|---|---|---|---|---|---|
| Status of Head and Household Number | Number of Persons in Household | Relation of Household Members to Head | Remarks | Born | Immig. | Emig. | Died |
| Child of Pueblo | | | | | | | |
| 13 ♀ | 1 | | Widow of vecino | | | | |
| 14* ♀ | 3 | H,D | | | | | |
| 15* ♀ | 4 | H,D,(S)* | | | | S | |
| 16* ♀ | 2 | H | | | | | |
| 17* ♂ | 2 | W | | | | | |
| Other | | | | | | | |
| 18* | 4 | W,S,D | With postal service | S | | | D |
| 19* | 5 | W,D,D,D | Railroad employee | | | S | |
| 20* | 1 | | Employee in Household 23 | | | | |
| 21* | 6 | W,S,D,WM,WB* | | | | | |
| 22* | 5 | W,S,S,S | Baker | | | | |
| 23* | 4 | W,D,D | Storekeeper; vecino of Aguasalida | | | | |
| 24* | 2 | W | Retired railroad worker; kin in station | | | W | H |
| 25* | 1 | | Baker's apprentice | | | ♂ | |
| 26* | | | Railroad employee | | H*,W,S | | |
| 27* | | | WZ of Household 17, widow | | ♀ | | |

NOTE: 1963 total population, 87; 1966 total population, 78. B = brother, D = daughter, F = father, H = husband, M = mother, S = son, W = wife, Z = sister.

Parentheses represent individuals living part-time out of pueblo.

Sex symbols represent sex of child of pueblo with reference to whom household members are listed.

* Individual or household head with salaried job.

wise employed by the postal service. In 1965 he emigrated to a full-time postal job in Pamplona. He chose not to enter the común, thus forfeiting his rights to the use of most communal resources. Therefore he was allowed no grazing rights for animals and no wood for fuel. His wife cooked with butane gas. In a previous era, such an adjustment would not have been possible, for a farm family could not have depended upon outside sources for its supply of meat or fuel. In 1963, this man kept one mule and borrowed one from one of his vecino brothers to complete the team. His animal, unlike his brother's, had grazing rights only on land which had been expropriated by the railroad and was under state rather than village jurisdiction.[2]

Común membership and residence in the village form the bases for ordering villagers' participation in a variety of contexts. To share responsibility and take equal turns is the rule of life in these small villages. The performance of certain ceremonial functions, the responsibility for performing certain tasks, the sharing of communally incurred expenses all fall equally upon vecino families. There are several mechanisms in use for insuring the smooth passage of responsibility from one family to the next. Sometimes households are ordered on the basis of their men's seniority in the común. A farmer formally enters the común de vecinos with the payment of a fee (or sometimes its equivalent in foodstuffs) when he begins actively to work an estate and establishes a separate household. The two bachelor vecinos in the Valdemora común are indeed active household heads as well as full-fledged farmers and have formally entered the común. For the others, entry into the común coincides with marriage. Marriage automatically defines a man as an adult farmer; a bachelor may be over the normal age of marriage before he is regarded as a confirmed bachelor and a

2. Dias (1953) explores the marginal position of fourteen families with respect to the closed corporate community of Rio de Onor (Tras-os-Montes), in Portugal. These families worked land resulting from estate-splitting in a region with a strong rule of estate impartibility; they were denied membership in the corporate community and owed their economic survival to the use of modern techniques which freed them from dependence upon the corporately controlled resources.

committed adult farmer. Until then, there is always the possibility of his marrying a woman with holdings elsewhere and moving away to farm them instead. The común wants members with a permanent commitment to Valdemora. In any case, Valdemorans rotate their ceremonial offices, to be described later, in order of the vecinos' seniority. When a young man marries, the order is broken and he is initiated into some of his ceremonial duties in the year of his marriage. Thereafter, he assumes his junior position at the end of the list. The junior vecino also traditionally fills the office of *alguacil* (see chapter 4) until a new member takes his place.

A more frequent method of rotating responsibilities is on the basis of vecinos' house order in the village. Beginning at an arbitrary starting point and following a fixed succession through the irregular village streets, some duties are handled in turn by the various families. This rotation is known as the *adra,* a word meaning "turn" deriving from the Arabic. A verb, *adrar,* which is never used in Valdemora, refers specifically to the rotation of irrigation rights, on whatever basis these are determined. The adra in Valdemora is always a rotation based on house order rather than any other kind of order, and it is the adra alone which also determines irrigation turns in the village. Documents point to the one-time rotation of irrigation turns on the basis of plot order, and this distinct ordering principle was called the *sortía.*[3] Villages differ in their use of the seniority and house-order principles for

3. The sortía, or plot-order rotation, is recorded in Valdemora only for purposes of irrigation and is no longer used. It is in use elsewhere in different contexts—for example, as a basis for ordering families' turns to thresh in Rio de Onor (Dias 1953). The term *sortía,* related to the word *suerte* for plot of land, is apparently not recognized by the Spanish Academy. It is not to be confused with the related (and recognized) term *sorteo,* meaning lottery and related to the more common use of the term *suerte* in reference to chance or fortune. The lottery, or sorteo, is in frequent use in the northern peninsula in the same contexts in which the auction occurs in Valdemora and elsewhere (see below). Sortía and sorteo may actually occur in combination, as in Rio de Onor, where families are assigned the use of threshing plots by lottery and threshing operations then proceed by plot order. House order and plot order may have been related in some parts of Europe, as evidenced by some of the data on Scandinavian settlements (summarized in Homans 1941, from a variety of sources).

different purposes—there may be shifts in use from one to the other in a village from time to time—but they remain the dominant principles of rotation within each común. In Valdemora, the adra is operative in most contexts—different types of responsibilities have independent adras—whereas the seniority principle functions primarily with respect to ceremonial offices, although this is not systematically true throughout the area. The adra, however, is more generally extended to a wider variety of duties than is the seniority rule, for an obvious reason. While rotation on the basis of común seniority must be confined to común households alone, the adra is a more flexible rule which permits the integration of non-común members where necessary. There is clear need for this flexibility in Valdemora.

The operation of the adra in Valdemora is not without amusing aspects. The común is so small that some of the occasions for which the adra is activated—such as gravedigging when a vecino household is bereaved—are very infrequent. Tradition stresses the careful recording of organizational bylaws, but not of the running accounts of action taken, with the result that often no one can remember "in which house the adra rests." The adra cannot always be reactivated at its proper starting-point, or duties would continually fall upon the same household. This situation calls for the activation of yet another traditional method of appropriating obligations—the drawing of lots, the *sorteo*. The drawing, then, determines which house shall take up the adra, and from that house, if records are kept, the rotation will continue by the traditional order. The sorteo is also the recognized means by which equal shares of property are assigned to individuals in a group of heirs to an estate. This use of the sorteo within the kin group also occurs in Greece.[4]

The común de vecinos functions to administer, through the council, the use of those resources and facilities which are defined as being communal and to insure mutual aid among its members.

4. Friedl 1964; Levy 1956.

In the latter sphere, some of its functions are explicitly focused on mobilization to meet crises and some are more difficult to identify at first glance. In some instances, the whole range of functions occurs together. In the following consideration of the común's activities I have included some which are no longer practiced, but about which there is documentation and often the testimony of older villagers. Some life-histories were collected in the field specifically to shed light on village customs which only recently fell into disuse. I describe the present and the past together here (but in different tenses) to give a more detailed view of the range of the común's activities. Although this range has narrowed or sometimes changed focus, the manner in which the común executes its business is the same. Aspects of many of these changes, including villagers' explanations of why they have taken place, will be specifically considered in chapters 6 and 7.

Three types of land are communally owned and exploited. Pasture *(pasto)* is the poor, hillside land on which the sheep are grazed. Meadow *(prado)* is the fertile, natural or cultivated grassland where draft animals are grazed and hay harvested for them. Some tracts of meadow were privately owned in the past, but they have long been cultivated in grain, leaving only the town common *(dehesa)*. This change is associated with the decreased dependence on cows for draft and the use of mules instead. Woodlands *(monte)* are the hillside areas, wooded with low scrub, of which rotating sectors are cut for fuel. There is historical evidence that the común once owned a few parcels of grainland, but this was no longer true in 1963.

Cultivated lands, which are privately owned, are opened to collective exploitation when the livestock of all families alike are allowed to graze on the stubble after the harvest. So that areas of stubble and of fallow may be of fairly continuous expanse, the council loosely coordinates the biennial rotation. Fields on one "side" of the municipality will be cultivated in one year and left fallow in the next. Farmers follow the general rule in a given year, though a few fields on the fallow side may be and always are cultivated as well. This is the only sense in which the corporate community traditionally functions to control farming activities, which are otherwise governed by individual families.

All of the sources of water in the village which are exploited for human use fall under public domain by national law. It is important that water-use is a social phenomenon in this part of Spain. (There are in the village some private sources of water which do not fall under public domain, but these are used by their owners for very limited purposes.) In addition to the surface streams from which water is diverted for irrigation, there is the spring, or town fountain *(fuente)*, where households draw their water and water their livestock. The fuente also feeds the public laundry-place *(lavadero)*. One annual meeting of the vecinos is devoted to the establishment of the irrigation adra. The turns amount to about one-half day per week per owner.

In addition to controlling the use of certain kinds of land and of the water supply, the común owns and administers the use of a variety of other properties. The village streets, the electric lights by which they are lighted at night, and the roads and paths between village and fields are all common property. Families are assessed equally for the cost of public electricity. The común is also responsible for heating the schoolhouse, although the building is government property. One building, formerly a house for the schoolteacher, is owned by the común, which collects rent whenever the house is occupied. The meetinghouse, the *ayuntamiento*, serving also as a dance hall for the younger generation, is común property, and the entire ground floor of this building houses the communal oven and bakery, now in disuse. At one time, the común owned a corral on the town common where the draft animals were sometimes sheltered. This is no longer in existence.

The cleaning and repair of all public facilities are shared in equally by the vecinos. In most instances the labor is performed by the men alone, but the semiweekly cleaning of the lavadero is performed in rotation by the women who use it, including some from nonfarm families. Occasions when the men join forces for work on communal properties are known as *cendera*. One day a year, Shrove Tuesday, is dedicated to this end; other days of cendera occur as needs dictate. When few participants are needed, vecinos are called by adra. The men also join to harvest the hay from the town common and to mark off plots of woodland within the area designated for exploitation in a given year. The latter is done with the ducal forester from Medinaceli.

There have been in Valdemora's documented history some public offices which it was the común's job to fill or to contract out. The two positions which were filled by villagers were those of cowherd *(vaquero)* and custodian of the oven *(hornero)*. The cowherd was responsible for grazing all of the town's draft animals on the town common during the months of heaviest work in the fields, generally from 24 June (San Juan) to 11 November (San Martín). This is a time during which families cannot spare extra labor for this purpose during the few hours when the animals are not in use. The ideal cowherd was an older vecino whose son had already taken over active farming or someone whose family had an unusually large labor force. In any case, the cowherds of whom we have record were usually natives of Valdemora and otherwise were villagers from the immediate area. They were appointed each year and paid by each family in proportion to the number of animals it sent to pasture. Occasionally a house-order adra was established which required families to send individuals to attend the draft animals for stated numbers of days; this happened when the job could not be filled in the usual way. Neither the position of cowherd nor the corral in the common exists today. By the beginning of this century most families were using mules rather than cows or oxen for draft; mules require less grazing and are stall-fed on oats much of the time. Although the last team of oxen was still in use in Valdemora as late as 1964, we have no record of a cowherd's contract later than 1899, and only older villagers remember the existence of such a position. The position of hornero, on the other hand, survived until the advent of the commercial bakery in town. The hornero was usually a man, and he usually remained in office for a year, firing the oven and helping the women to take their loaves in and out of it on the weekly baking day. Occasionally, according to one old woman, the duties of hornero were filled by adra, and she herself remembers taking the turn for her household when her husband was sick. More often, however, an auction was held and the position was awarded to the highest bidder for a year's time. The nature of such auctions will be discussed presently. A further item of common business was the disposition of the ashes from the oven and the manure from the village streets and communal corral, all for fertilizer. These were also auctioned in the village.

Until quite recently the común employed a volunteer from the pueblo as field guard on the summer nights before the grain harvest (from April to August or September). This man reported the entry into the fields of any grazing animals, and the owners were subsequently fined. The guard's job was considered more important in the days when flocks from other villages were permitted to cross municipal boundaries. Today this is prohibited, and the Valdemora shepherds feel enough responsibility for their own village's fields that the guard is no longer necessary. The last guards in memory were paid for the season's work one *peseta* for each animal owned in the municipality. Part of the money from fines was sometimes paid them also, but most of this was applied toward the expenses of the feast of San Roque.

The council traditionally contracted with outsiders for services which no one in Valdemora was equipped to perform. Thus, documents relate dealings with a teacher-sacristan, whose two functions are today filled separately by a teacher and a priest and paid by the government. Formerly, the duties of the sacristan were paid by communal subscription; those of teacher were paid by each family in proportion to the number and ages of the children it sent to school. Finally, two documents record contracts for the services of doctors from nearby towns. Today all families alike subscribe to a government-sponsored medical plan which gives the village the regular services of a doctor from Medinaceli. An arrangement which is still made today is the yearly contract with an itinerant dealer in lavender, to whom the común sells the right to collect lavender from the communal lands in the late summer. These men travel from village to village, collecting the plant and processing it in each place, selling some of the essence to village women and carrying away the surplus. Another dealing with the outside which the común still effects is the payment of rent on communal lands to the House of Medinaceli. Families are assessed for their shares and the amount is collected on the day of San Antonio, 13 June, every year, when the council also makes internal financial adjustments in connection with stubble-grazing.

The común mobilizes its members for purposes of giving mutual aid and protecting single members from excessive outside demands. This kind of community action is well documented for other villages in Spain and Portugal, especially in the north of the peninsula.[5] Giving charity to destitute members of the community, or food to fighting troops, as mentioned, is conceived as a burden on the community to be borne by all vecinos equally. Valdemorans used to feed and house itinerant beggars by adra when such people passed through town. Many aspects of charity-giving are informal in Valdemora in contrast to their more formal nature elsewhere.[6] The inhabitants of such a small village automatically help one another build houses, extinguish fires, and attend to illnesses, and in this they are bound by ties of kinship as well as common residence. Nonetheless, mutual aid most often is governed by formal rules. There was formerly among vecinos a *contrata de caballería,* or contract governing team animals, which bound all vecinos to contribute to the purchase of a new animal for any vecino who suffered loss through circumstances beyond his control. Unamuno records similar arrangements governing the care and insurance of

5. Cf. especially Costa 1902; Costa et al. 1902; Dias 1948 and 1953; and summary in Freeman 1968b.

6. Cf. especially Unamuno 1902.

cattle in the province of Vizcaya.[7] In Valdemora, stock insurance is now covered by more general insurance plans.

There was in Valdemora a communal granary, the *pósito pío,* of which we have good records from the nineteenth century only. The formal establishment of these rural credit funds in Spain probably had roots in government action of more than a single era. The documents which relate to Valdemora's pósito are all renderings of accounts to outside powers. We do know that grain theft by troops was deducted from the granary's holding; we know, too, that individuals did receive loans from the pósito during its recorded history. But we also know that members of the común came to one another's aid in times of need without recourse to a pósito (see, for example Appendix, sec. 3, Miscellaneous: 1857 record of donation). A modern example of the pooling of collective labor for each vecino in turn is very young in Valdemora. The members of the común joined in 1965 to purchase a threshing machine. Where single families had always threshed alone with a flint-toothed tribulum *(trillo)* drawn by mules, now threshing has become a focus of communal effort. The machine is operated at the expense of the común, and the vecinos attend to the threshing of each other's grain.

As I have said, most of the formal business of the común, such as the filling of contracts, the establishment of the irrigation schedule, and the assessment of fees is actually conducted among the men alone who, in this context, call themselves the concejo, or town council. Their officers are the *alcalde,* the *teniente alcalde* (vice-alcalde), the *tercero* (third), and the *alguacil* (aide). These positions exist largely with reference to the formal requirements of civil government (see chapter 4) and, with the exception of alguacil, do not rotate by traditional means, nor does the común invest them with any authority. Council meetings are not attended by women, even by widows who may have control over large portions of estates. The council is indeed composed only of

7. Unamuno 1902.

active farmers: retired vecinos often do not attend meetings if a married son represents the estate as its active farmer. A family sometimes sends two men to meetings if the son is not yet married and the father is still active.

In some contexts the común does not function through the council at all, but mobilizes under different names. Thus, there are two organizations, the brotherhood honoring the patron saint, the Hermandad de San Isidro (Brotherhood of San Isidro) and the burial society, the Hermandad de Nuestro Señor (Brotherhood of Our Lord), which are conceived to be corporately distinct from the común de vecinos, but whose membership is virtually identical. The male members of these groups meet regularly, but in these contexts the body is not known as the concejo; to the male segment of each group attach offices which are entirely distinct from those of the concejo. Valdemorans view the Hermandad de San Isidro, to be described in chapter 4, as a strictly ceremonial organization with no overt functions. The burial society will be considered here as an organization for mutual aid.

The burial society has left thorough records of its affairs over the past century and has, quite obviously, an unwritten history as well. Similar societies are active in villages throughout the region. Membership is usually attained by married couples, who pay a joint entrance fee and, thereafter, separate annual dues for both husband and wife. Entrance is "voluntary" at the time of being married or of becoming a vecino, but there is an additional charge if entry is delayed after this time. Members are required to attend certain masses and vespers during the year and to attend funeral masses of all individuals who are *hermanos* or members of their families. Fines are levied for failure to attend any of these. The society underwrites the expenses of burial and the maintenance of the cemetery. The fifty-year maintenance of grave sites costs members a total of 250 pesetas.[8] All members must bring candles to funeral masses and masses dedicated to the burial society and

8. One dollar was the equivalent of sixty pesetas until November 1967, when the official rate of exchange was altered to seventy pesetas per dollar.

are fined for failure to do so. The funeral masses referred to are the *misas de cuerpo presente*, the preburial masses for which the coffin is brought into the church. Commemorative masses after the burial and novenas at the home of the deceased are the responsibilities of the family involved and do not require the attendance of the entire society. The obligations of membership also require the attendance of hermanos at the bedsides of gravely ill members; the obligation is enforced from the point at which the sacraments have been administered, or when the patient's family requests assistance. The bonds of sentiment in the village often make enforcement of the rules unnecessary, but regulations call for activation of the adra in attending the sick, and in cases of prolonged illness representatives of only two households are present each day. Keeping the wake with the family of the deceased, which in this region is a solemn vigil unmarked by feasting or singing, is mentioned in older documents as falling by adra to two members of the society at a time, but there is little need to enforce this rule—the entire village generally attends a bereaved family.

The burial society has two officers, called the senior and junior *mayordomos* or *piostres*. These offices are held by male members in the order of their seniority in the organization. The seniority ranking is not identical to the order in which people entered the común. Individuals whose parents are alive and members of the organization do not join unless they marry, establishing new households and requiring coverage for their wives. A bachelor vecino does not enter the burial society while one of his parents still lives; Valdemora's two bachelor vecinos differ in this respect and, accordingly, one of them is not yet a member.

A consideration of the mutual-aid functions of the común would be incomplete without reference to the traditions which, until the recent past, surrounded the redistribution of meat in the community. The possession of even a small flock of sheep was as crucial for a family's subsistence as are the irrigable plots which produce vegetables for the table. The Spanish word for meat, *carne*, in the villages of this region refers only to lamb or mutton. Other flesh foods are called by the names of the animals from which they come—cow, bull, calf, pig, goat, etc.—and, except for pork, rabbit, and domesticated fowl, are all luxury items available only through the market. The flocks of sheep traditionally represented the family's source of wool as well as its supply of meat. Very few women still spin wool, and then only for knitting and not weaving cloth. Almost all clothing has been store-bought for many years. The dependence upon the market system for fresh lamb is much more recent and some families still slaughter their own animals at times. The nature of changes in this respect will be discussed later, but change is quite recent. In 1963 six of the ten vecinos kept sheep, though now largely for the market. In 1966 only three vecinos still had large flocks and two kept a few animals.

The slaughter of a lamb makes available more meat than any nuclear-family household can consume before spoilage, and the nuclear-family household is the largest commensal unit in daily village life. People circumvent the problem of surplus today by purchasing small quantities of meat daily from the butcher. In the past, the problem of preserving surplus meat was sometimes solved by salting and hanging parts of the animal. Only one old woman still remembers the procedure and virtually everyone else in town declares it a custom best buried: the nearly universal opinion is that pork products are the only ones which are not worsened by preservation. Winter is the only season in which the preservation can be begun without ill effects. Whereas the hams processed then improve with age, some informants say the salt-mutton tends to spoil in summer or, at least, to taste more disagreeable than ever. Families did in the past hang lamb for their winter consumption but did not supply their summer needs in this way. Even if the meat did last, a large-scale sheep slaughter would severely reduce the breeding stock and limit wool production. Many factors thus militated against storage and in favor of some other mechanism for regularizing meat consumption. Valdemora's written history gives ample evidence of one of the ways in which the problem was solved; that is, by redistributing meat from a slaughter throughout the community, so that all families received manageable amounts of fresh meat. Such redistribution was often effected through the auctions which occurred in the context of handling certain items of común business already mentioned.

The auctions of which we have records (dating from the last century) are those in which vecinos bid competitively for the special benefits and products proceeding from communal properties: ashes from the oven and manure from the communal streets and corral, all for fertilizer; the right to cultivate bits of communal land which were not otherwise destined for use in a given year; and the right to be hornero for a year. (Hornero was a desirable position for anyone who could give up one day each week: he was paid in bread and thus could market the year's bread-wheat otherwise required for his family's consumption.) Here is one of the recorded examples of the auction procedure:

> In the town of Valdemora on the eighth of December, 1883 . . . the use of the produce [ash] of the bakery oven for the year of 1884 was auctioned under the following conditions. . . .
>
> Pedro Sancho placed the bid at . . . one lamb of good worth for the day of the auction. Francisco Romanillos raised the bid one small package of tobacco for each vecino for the day of the auction. Pascual del Barrio raised it a half *arroba* of fried fish for the day of Candlemas [2 February] with the condition that whoever is not present loses his share, barring the case of sickness. Pedro Sancho raised it one *arroba* of wine for Candlemas. Francisco Romanillos raised it twenty *reales* [currency]. José Riosalido raised it one lamb of good worth for the Octava del Señor [1 January]. Pascual del Barrio raised it one *real* for each vecino. . . . It went to Pascual del Barrio for the quantities mentioned.[9]

9. See Appendix, sec. 3. This archive indicates that the town council in the last half of the past century had an unusual bent for recording its own acts. Informants' memories of later periods and indirect references in earlier periods corroborate the existence of the same traditions in periods when the council did not leave as many written records.

Documents like this illustrate that the bidding in these auctions dealt heavily in foodstuffs, particularly the protein foods which are the preferred main courses in the ideal meal. Although lambs were almost always bid, such items as fish, cheese, wine, and tobacco often entered the picture as well. The typical auction procedure established one or more dates on which the slaughtered animal, or animals, and other items were to be consumed. The single auction recorded above established dates for three separate feasts—the day of the auction itself, Candlemas, and New Year's Day. The fact that many of the dates specified in such records fall in the winter months indicates that people did not rely entirely on salt-mutton even in winter. The religious aspects of such feasts will be discussed later, but here it is important to point out that the auction system established a calendar of events in the village that solved for individual families the problem of providing their tables with manageable quantities of meat without wastage and without drastically depleting the numbers of their breeding stock by large-scale slaughtering for storage. The común de vecinos functioned as a meat-sharing society in the course of performing some of its other business. Animals were also slaughtered by the vecinos on occasions other than those specified at auctions—this is still done on the day of San Antonio (see chapter 4) and in the past probably at other specified times as well. Furthermore, there appear to have been informal arrangements among vecinos to share in lamb slaughters simply when they needed meat. The widow Josefa, the only living advocate of salt-mutton, describes the situation at the turn of the century as follows:

> There were no butchers. We'd kill an animal and salt it; it hung to dry and made a good *cocido* [the local chick-pea stew]. We dried it just like salt-pork. It lasts just as long as you like—in the right weather, but in summer it doesn't. In summer you know what we did? Well, I'd kill a lamb; someone would take half and I'd take half. And when we finished that lamb he'd kill one and return the meat to me. So in summer we didn't have to store it. A vecino would likely tell you, "Well, go on then, you slaughter a lamb today, give me some, and tomorrow or the day after I'll slaughter." That lasted two

> or three days; then the other person would slaughter. In summertime you use more—you've got harvest hands and you need more, so we did it that way.

In the harvest season two families could indeed consume an animal in two or three days. At other times, these informal arrangements involved a greater number of families and appear to have assumed the dimensions of village feasts.

The ethnography of meat sharing in Spain is an involved and fascinating subject. Here it is enough to point out that it is very frequently a corporate function—corporate villages or corporate subdivisions within villages have been reported to feast together in a wide variety of contexts.[10] There are reports from some localities of corporations which formed for the explicit purpose of sharing meat and establishing rotating obligations to slaughter animals, and of some town councils which ran slaughterhouses and butcher shops to serve the entire community.[11] The social pleasures of feasting have in many instances led people to pursue these traditions in an era in which the cooperative redistribution of meat is no longer a necessity. There are fewer auctions and feasts on Valdemora's calendar today than there were in the last century, but we can see in them the traces of redistributive processes. Valdemorans, who are quite aware of the more extensive functions of the feasts in the recent past, maintain the last of

10. The phenomenon of corporate commensal events is by no means confined to rural Spain. In the capital city of Soria, the men of the confraternities which sponsor the bullfights and other events of the city's famous fiesta of San Juan gather as groups to cook and eat their respective bulls. The group's culinary efforts are competitive and are submitted to a jury of officials, who taste of each *caldera* (cauldron). Farther north, men's culinary societies function in Basque country, especially in urban centers. These groups form specifically for commensal purposes and may meet as often as once a week. Some usually visit favorite eating places together; others do their own cooking, collect recipes, and sometimes own or rent their own meeting premises. As women are strictly excluded from these functions, the wives of "society men" may form their own groups, with each other or with friends, to dine together on "society night."

11. Costa 1898, pp. 319–21, 561–62; Serrano Gómez 1902, pp. 388–89; Costa et al. 1902, pp. 389–90 n.

these traditions with a conscious effort, explicitly "so as not to lose the custom," insisting at the same time that pueblo traditions are bound to die.

The común de vecinos of a single village has in the past united with those of other villages for certain purposes. The interests which bound villages together in the Sierra Ministra frequently centered on sheepherding and, in particular, on the maintenance of their sheep pastures. The focus of communal concerns on problems of sheepherding and pasturage is an ancient phenomenon in Spain and throughout the Mediterranean. In Spain, these concerns enter written history as early as the sixth and seventh centuries, in the codes of the Visigoths. Attention was centered from an early period on the regulation of long-range transhumant flocks—on the establishment of sheepwalks, branding regulations, rules for the disposal of strays, and the separation of the realm of jurisdiction of the transhumant herders from that of the villagers, that is, farmers and nontranshumant stock breeders, whose territories were periodically traversed. The incorporation of Castilian sheepherders under a formal charter in 1273; the rise of this organization, the Honrado Concejo de la Mesta, to a position of enormous power under Ferdinand and Isabela in the early sixteenth century; and its eventual decline are the subject of Julius Klein's classic in institutional history.[12] The herding of merino sheep for their superior wool had become, by some time in the early Middle Ages, the basis of a full-time occupation in certain parts of northern Old Castile and León. Merino herding became the basis of Spain's wool industry, in which she gained world ascendency and maintained a successful monopoly until merino flocks were established in northern Europe in the early eighteenth century. The Crown's interest in the wool trade brought the Mesta to focus on the affairs of the migrant herders, and local herders' traditions are less well documented for those centuries and their interests were far less well protected.

12. Klein 1920.

In the Medinaceli region, what we know of the town leagues for pasturage comes from the ducal archives, and most of the references to these organizations are indirect. The town leagues to which references exist, however, are known to have parallels in other parts of Old Castile, where a few survive today,[13] and in Aragón, where they were larger and more resistant to pressure from such sources as the Mesta.[14] Some of the terms applied to the units of such organizations and to their officers are used widely enough in the peninsula, in pastoral and other contexts, to suggest that many features of local organization were formalized in, rather than originated by, the Mesta charter.

The town leagues, or cuadrillas, of the Sierra Ministra were groupings of about twenty villages with contiguous municipal boundaries. Valdemora joined with sixteen neighboring towns in the Cuadrilla de Calzada. The member towns elected at least one joint official, called alcalde of the mesta or alcalde of the corral, and provided continuous expanses of pasture for entry by the flocks of any family of a member town during the summer pasturage season (from May to November). No other details of the cuadrilla's activities are known. The most recent reference to its existence is dated in 1717, and Valdemorans in 1963 were unaware that such an organization had ever existed. The joining of village pastures assured that members' flocks would be able to graze even if their own village pastures suffered from natural disaster. Valdemorans do recall a period when shepherds crossed village lines, but today this is prohibited. Distances militate against the consistent entry of one village's flocks into the pastures of all the other cuadrilla villages. Today no shepherd sleeps in the

13. Professor Julio González of the Faculty of History in the University of Madrid, on the basis of his extensive familiarity with Castilian archives, was able to corroborate the existence of such organizations over a wide area. He knew of the existence of some town leagues in the province of Ávila as late as 1963, at which time he also told me that no description of these organizations was to be found in print. Since then, Valdeavellano (1968) has offered a very brief description of medieval pasturage leagues.

14. Klein 1920.

pastures, and the daily return to the village is what people feel distinguishes their shepherd-kinsmen from the class of professional herders whom they consider their social inferiors.

Many of the data examined above point to the importance of a summer season, be it for pasturage or meat sharing. The pressures of this season—the season of heavy farm labor—appear to be two in kind: first, more food is consumed and, second, there is less manpower available for the performance of nonagricultural tasks. The first factor appears to have encouraged a variety of meat-sharing procedures in that season, and the second led a village like Valdemora to pasture its draft animals with a single man. With the disappearance of the office of vaquero, there is no longer any noticeable distinction between summer and winter herding practices. This change accompanies the advent of mule-drawn machinery which eased the pressures of the harvest season: by 1963 the practice of hiring migrant harvest hands was also almost dead, and by 1966 two tractors had dramatically reduced the pressures and completely freed women from harvest duties in the fields. When we look back to the era in which the cuadrilla existed, it is not unreasonable to ask if town leagues might not have functioned to contract shepherd-labor for the families of member towns, releasing the family herdsmen for work in the fields. Present practices alone offer no explanation for the careful maintenance of the May–November season mentioned in all the documents. The approximate date on which Valdemora still pays its annual rent to the House of Medinaceli is 11 November, though the sum is collected on 13 June (San Antonio). All towns in the cuadrilla owed similar rents in Medinaceli, and it is traditional throughout the area to collect these on the same day. It is not improbable that the cuadrillas once dealt as units with the Duchy; this might explain why some reports of their joint activities are found in the ducal archives.

There exists in the Valdemora region today an organization called the Hermandad del Cabildo (Brotherhood of the Council House), which is the only extant example of a town league bearing any relation to sheep herding (though it also functions as a burial society). Its nature is suggestive of the possible roles such an organization might have played in an earlier period and in this sense it deserves mention along with the cuadrilla. The Hermandad del Cabildo has its center in the village of Salcedo. Membership is voluntary and includes vecinos of several villages. These pay an entrance fee of one lamb per married couple. The livestock capital (about one hundred lambs in 1963) is divided into groups of ten, called cuadrillas. Every five years members bid in auction for the right to keep one of the cuadrillas until the next auction. The winning bidders breed, kill, or sell the animals as they wish, but must produce ten young animals for the next auction. The proceeds of the auction are used to pay the keepers of cuadrillas for expenses and to provide a special mass and feast for all members on San Martín, 11 November, the date of the official end of the summer pasturage season throughout the Sierra Ministra. Such an organization may once have solved the problem of pasturing and caring for a herd for which many families or villages had joint responsibility; or of pasturing a jointly owned herd which was conceived as a "butcher-shop on the hoof" for its owners' consumption.[15] It can also be viewed as a form of capital investment insuring stock owners against losses occurring in their own localities by dispersing the capital over a wide area.

Whatever their functions may have been, corporate organizations on the intervillage level were apparently active in the Sierra

15. Serrano Gómez (1902, pp. 388–89) notes the custom of the town councils' "obligation" to support a communal butchering enterprise in the villages in the Soria-Burgos-Logroño border. Here, the right to be butcher was auctioned annually. The winning bidder bought weak and poor stock from all villagers at a low price and was given the exclusive right to fatten them on a select tract of communal pasture. He was then obliged to slaughter and sell meat as the vecinos required it, for no more than the standard price of the season. This enterprise operated during the summer months (June to September or later).

Ministra in the past, and it would be wrong to view the village as the largest unit of the indigenous social organization. Today, however, most of the old forms of insurance society have been replaced and the only extant examples of town leagues are voluntary associations, largely ceremonial in function.[16] Another extant league centers in Valdemora's neighbor town of Molinos: this is a confraternity honoring the Virgin of Quintanares. Membership is compulsory for vecinos of Molinos, among whom the offices of the three chief mayordomos rotate by house order, but vecinos of several other towns as well are voluntary members, and each town with members also has one mayordomo. The organization functions solely with respect to the two feast days that honor the Virgin. Interestingly, these feasts occur in early June and in late September, near the end-points of the critical season for both farming and herding in the region.

The council of adult men is not the only corporate subdivision of the común de vecinos. Other groups, defined along lines of both sex and age (or marital status),[17] assume specific functions in village life and tend to become particularly active in ceremonial contexts. As in the común itself, membership in its subdivisions never crosses village lines, but is territorially exclusive.

The first formal separation of the sexes occurs at the age of five or six and corresponds closely with children's entry into the school

16. The response to the Ateneo questionnaire of 1901 (Ateneo 1901) from the town of Lumbrales (Salamanca) reports the existence of a burial society with membership from a number of towns.

17. The description of these groups which follows makes evident that they are not really "age groups," though I call them that simply as a matter of convenience. I know of no term which fits the present type. People do not enter or leave the ranks together; rather, the individual's passage from one group to another occurs with his arrival at certain points of the life cycle, such as his seventeenth birthday or his wedding day. The corporation (sometimes called a *gremio*, or guild) claims as its members all individuals of one sex who have passed the point of entry and have not yet reached the point for passage into the next group.

system, followed shortly by the celebration of first communion. Until this time, children of both sexes play together; afterward they do not. This change, unlike later ones, is not accompanied by a change in the terms used to describe this age group. Children are called *niños* (boys) and *niñas* (girls) from about the time they begin to walk. Before this they are *críos* (male babies) or *crías* (female babies). It is not until three years after the end of compulsory schooling, at age fourteen, that niños and niñas become *mozos* (young bachelors) and *mozas* (maidens). These terms are applied very carefully in Valdemora only to people approaching or past their seventeenth birthdays. The terms *chicos* and *chicas* may apply to a broader age range of boys or girls, or even young married people, but a fifteen-year-old girl is still only "almost a moza." The male's passage from niño to mozo is most unequivocally marked by the requirement that, at age seventeen, he pay for formal entry into the corporation of village mozos.[18] In recent years, the entrance fee was set as high as three hundred pesetas. The mozos of Valdemora have recently been accepting the substitution of foodstuffs for cash payment: the new entrant into the group invites all the mozos to a snack or to a drinking party. The small size of the group assures that the bill for such an event does not exceed three hundred pesetas.

To be no longer niños is to be marriageable; to be a mozo or moza is, by definition, to be able to court. By tradition, the mozas of a town are intended for the mozos of the same town. The extent to which this is impossible in a village as small as Valdemora will be examined later. The group of mozos is ritually involved in upholding the reputation of its town against foreign mozos and in exacting its due if a foreigner assumes the prerogative of a native mozo by courting a native girl. A moza with a *novio*

18. Compare the data on León (López Morán 1902), where niños aged seven to sixteen *(niños rapaces)* often form a more clearly corporate group than they do in Valdemora. Mozos' entrance fees are paid in wine. In some parts of the region, mozas as well pay entrance fees.

*forastero* (outsider-boyfriend) finds weeds and brambles, rather than flowers, by her door on the morning of San Juan, left there by the mozos of her village who, when she marries the forastero, will exact from him a fee.[19]

When a mozo marries, he becomes a *casado*. Only some of the mozos pay the fee, or provide the feast, for entry into the común, and any nonfarmer who continues to live in the village as a casado is simply a child of the pueblo, but has no corporate membership. In speaking of men's corporate groups, therefore, it is correct to speak only of vecinos and not of casados. When the married women, *casadas*, function together by virtue of their membership in the común de vecinos, their number is strictly limited to the wives of vecinos. They are sometimes referred to as *las mujeres*, specifically, the wives of the común, though the term is also used in reference to any adult females. In most villages of the area, with rare non-vecino residents, the terms *vecino* and *mujer* embrace the entire adult population. In Valdemora, no terminology has developed to distinguish the adult females of the común from those of the railroad settlement, and people must continually clarify their references to the común members.

Almost all of the vecinos' wives come from different villages. As housewives and mothers in the pueblo, wives of vecinos share much of their daily round with non-común wives. Their farmer-husbands, by definition, have few daily activities in common with salaried non-vecinos. The group of wives of the común tends to extend its boundaries to include outsiders more often than does the group of farmers. One of the leaders of the women's group is an artisan's wife, a daughter of the pueblo, but no longer a común

19. The custom of charging outsiders for courting or marrying village girls is widespread, but the only region where a name for the fee has been recorded is the Sierra de Béjar (on the Ávila-Cáceres-Salamanca border), where the fee is called *el pijardo*. The term is reported by Stanley Brandes of the University of California at Berkeley (personal communication), who says that Béjar mozos speak of "charging pijardo" *(cobrando pijardo)*. Valdemorans simply say "we charge" and have no name for the fee.

wife. The greater strength of the corporate ties binding vecinos, in contrast to their wives, is reflected in the fact that the term *forastero* (a person from any other village) marks male outsiders from male insiders but is not often used to separate females in the same way. The significant point here is that the común de vecinos always and systematically incorporates women from other villages, while it includes forastero men only rarely and in special circumstances. The locus of continuity in the population lies only in the corporation of vecinos and never in the group of wives. Accordingly, the mozas are always bound for membership in their husbands' communities, and the core of the group of mozos of Valdemora shares a common future as vecinos. The degree to which foreign females are continually being integrated differs in larger communities where endogamous matches are more common and many mozas become casadas in their native villages.[20]

People of like sex and age range or marital status perform many activities as groups, and some activities are defined as falling within the specific provinces of different groups. In the daily work round, the activities of the sexes are more clearly separate than are those of any subdivisions within them. Mozas will be at the lavadero with their mothers, older girls will be responsible for watching younger ones, mozos and older niños may work with their fathers in the fields, and so on. But even on this level there is a noticeable tendency for association within the age-based subdivisions; informal associations for certain purposes consistently cross household lines. This is most true for females, whose daily activities are largely in the village where contacts are closer. Thus, mozas often do their families' shopping together, go to the fountain for water or to the station on errands together, and embroider together, with their mothers, at their house doors in the after-

20. A household census of four of Valdemora's larger neighbors shows a consistently higher proportion of households in which man and wife are both natives, and this proportion increases systematically with absolute population size.

noon.[21] The significant point is not that mozas help their mothers by running errands, which is hardly surprising, but that they use many of these activities specifically for associational purposes, fixing times of meeting and calling at each other's houses in order to be able to run their errands as a group.

A variety of occasions are culturally defined as times for socializing across household lines.[22] (These will be more fully examined in chapter 4.) The more formal the occasion, the sharper become the lines separating age groups from one another. Thus, on Sunday afternoons, which are culturally defined as times of village-wide relaxation, mozas and casadas are not to be found embroidering together. Rather, the mozas take long walks together in the hills while their mothers gather in the small plaza for their weekly card game. A moza is never found near the card table for any length of time: this is the realm of married women and the young children whom they must watch. School-age boys and girls are to be found roaming the village in separate groups. Mozos

21. There is in Valdemora no *hilandera* (women's spinning or sewing circle) as inclusive and formal as those of northwestern Spain (Costa et al. 1902). Where casadas and mozas meet formally in fixed localities, the hilanderas may become the focus of the mozos' nightly social round and the married women serve as chaperones at the meeting of the unmarried people. Sanders (1949) describes the same situation in a Bulgarian village.

22. Again, the same tendency exists all over rural and urban Spain, though its expression is often more informal than it is in Valdemora. In public places and in certain situations, it is customary for married women to form groups separately from their husbands, unmarried girls and bachelors group separately with their peers, and so on. Quite aside from the notion that certain activities are appropriate to only one of the sexes, men and women and different age groups also tend to separate when they are doing the same thing, especially if it is in public. This used to be true of seating patterns in church even in cities, though this has changed in cities in recent generations. Such separation is still strongly evident in cafés, where the taking of *merienda* (afternoon or evening snack) or an afternoon cup of coffee might be considered the national pastime. At one time, only men frequented cafés, and women gathered in less public places; today men and women form sharply separate groups on the same premises. It is relatively "modern" among the middle classes for groups of married or engaged couples to meet or go out together.

go together for a drink at the bar, where they drink separately from their fathers.

In the yearly schedule of feasts which are high points in Valdemora's social life, the male and female age-groups have specific roles. The niñas are responsible for singing the mass on Sundays. The mozas are occasionally responsible for singing special masses, such as the Easter mass. Mozos have special duties in fiesta processions, as do niños in one fiesta. Both seating-order in the church and marching-order in processions separate the two sexes and the three subdivisions of each.

The traditional aspects of the feast cycle, outside the context of the mass itself, activate these separate groups even further. For the feast of the patron saint, the mozos go into the hills to select a good oak bough for decoration. The vecinos, under the leadership of the year's mayordomo, collect the families' contributions toward the production of special cakes, which the mayordomo's wife is responsible for making. The vecinos run the auction of cakes and oak-bough. The mozas have recently been given a role here as well (see chapter 4). On San Antonio the vecinos feast together after the settlement of pastoral accounts. On San Roque, vecinos and their wives have separate wine-drinking parties in the afternoon and later join in a dance with the entire común. This feast once activated four mayordomos annually, rotating by house order, who supplied bread and cheese for all present, but this became quite expensive and the "Charity of San Roque" is no longer distributed. On San Juan it is traditional for mozos and mozas to go as separate groups into the hills to brew hot chocolate at dawn. On Todos los Santos, 1 November, the mozas gather to make a special honey confection, choosing by lottery the kitchen in which they will work. They then gather with the group of mozos in the meeting hall to eat the *gachas*. Jueves Lardero, the Thursday preceding Ash Wednesday, is again a day on which younger people go in groups for a *merienda* (elaborate afternoon or evening snack) in the hills. On the day of cendera—the repairing of communal properties on Shrove Tuesday—

the vecinos and the mozos, who have worked together, join for separate suppers. Each vecino brings a fixed portion of food (eggs and salt-pork) from home and the group cooks together. The mozos traditionally beg as a group from house to house, collecting the same foodstuffs and cooking them together. On the night before Easter, after an evening mass, the mozos unite to buy a merienda and then join efforts to make an effigy of Judas to hang in the street. The next morning it falls to the niños as a group to pull down and burn the effigy. The mozos are responsible for providing music for dances. They select a small band for the two major fiestas of the year and pay the musicians' fee. For lesser occasions, including the regular Sunday afternoon dances, it is the mozos who own and operate the village phonograph and record collection.

Strict boundaries are maintained between age groups in the formal activities listed above. Thus, though a thirty-five-year-old man may actively farm his father's land and attend some council meetings in his father's place, he performs with the mozos in ceremonial contexts until he is married or until his father dies. Although he may attend business meetings of the council, only his father attends the council's ceremonial feasts, such as that of San Antonio. Similarly, a moza whose marriage is impending will be invited to join married women's informal conversation groups, and these even perform some role in sex education. The content of much of the married women's talk and joking changes abruptly with the approach of unattached mozas, but those who have reached the last stages of courtship are admitted into the circle. In any formal event, however, no moza joins the activities of the casadas until after her wedding. Although people in their daily behavior recognize many stages of gradual "growing-up," the individual's progress from one status to another in ceremonial contexts is marked by sharp breaks.

Niños and niñas as groups have little to do with one another. The formal meeting of the sexes begins at age seventeen. The defining characteristic of mozos and mozas is that they are marriageable, and they meet as groups in the same ceremonial contexts in which other groups remain apart. Thus, on San Juan, though the two groups go into the hills separately for their breakfast of chocolate, they remain within shouting distance of each other and the distance lessens as the morning passes. Similarly, the mozas' honey gachas are eaten by both groups together on 1 November. Meetings of mozos and mozas assume the air of public performances played out before the rest of the community. For two hours on Sunday afternoons, they dance together in the meetinghouse. Watching the dance and trying to disrupt it forms the afternoon's entertainment for the groups of niños and niñas. The boys and girls carry on a battle with the priest, who has decreed that children should not observe dancing until they have passed their sixteenth birthdays. The dancers combat the outside noise with bursts of volume from the phonograph. The niños and niñas, while they are not being chased by the priest, perform the function of announcing to the whole village who is dancing with whom. Were the priest aware of the children's efficacy in the field of social control, he might allow them to stay and watch. Mozos and mozas generally give their attentions equally to all members of the other group. When one couple has danced together often over a period of several weeks, there is cause for general comment. Although almost all *noviazgos* begin at dances, favored partners are not regarded as becoming serious until they continue to favor one another over many months and begin making the *paseo* together. The paseo up and down the road begins at the meetinghouse after the dance and lasts until dark or the supper hour. Mozos and mozas walk as separate groups, circling near one another and calling back and forth. A fully engaged couple is allowed relative privacy; tentative new partnerships form in full public view and these couples are not allowed the release of sitting down together off the side of the road. A full paseo occurs only on Sundays and fiestas; only committed novios stroll together on other evenings.

Were the Valdemora dance populated solely by común people, it would be a miserable failure. The mozos and mozas of the común include young people from other families in many of their activities. In 1963 there were only four mozos in the común and their ranks were increased by a few young men from the station barrio. There were three mozas in the común, two who lived in the pueblo in families of children of the pueblo, and the storekeeper's daughter. There were five común niños and three sons of the non-vecino farmer. There were also five niñas in the común and the three daughters of a pueblo-dwelling railroad worker (Household 19, table 2). Non-común youth is excluded most often from the group of mozos, whose corporate organization is strongest. The dance is open to anyone of the right age, but its steadiest attendance is from the pueblo people who form the organizing core of the mozo and moza groups.

If the public confrontation of the sexes in the village conforms to strict patterns, the confrontation of mozos across village lines does so as well and is, in addition, highly competitive. Mozos and mozas have, and are expected to have, more extensive "foreign relations" than anyone else in the village. Where villages are so small, contacts must be sought in other communities, and village fiestas, with their dances, are the primary events of premarital social life in the Sierra Ministra. Mozos and mozas exploit a wide range of kinsmen in other villages as hosts for these occasions. Valdemora mozas are boarded separately in another village, but they make their excursion as a group and keep close contact during their visit. It is not necessary to have lodging in the two closest neighbor towns, less than an hour's walk away, and the Valdemora mozas tend to go and return as a group on each of the one or two most important days of the fiestas.

Girls cross village lines with relative ease and no fanfare; they are not foreigners in the fullest sense. The arrival of a group of mozos from another town on the scene of a fiesta establishes, by contrast, a state of ritual siege. The mozas are busy dancing with everyone but their usual Sunday partners. The mozos of different villages face each other as members of competing corporations whose rights to their own females are being challenged by outsiders.[23] The town fountain, the geographic focus of village life and symbol of corporate property ownership, is quite the right place to throw a forastero. For mozos, the calendar year of village fiestas is a calendar of practical jokes, competitive drinking and songfests, and real and alleged mass dunkings. The dilemma of the mozo lies in his need to enter foreign territory to find a wife in order to achieve the status of vecino at home. The bachelor years are the years of foreign wars. They culminate in the payment of a fee; traditionally a two-day wedding; and the return as a casado —a married man and a householder—to membership in the town council and management of the family estate.

Valdemora differs from most of its neighbors in two respects. Its small size places it at one extreme of the range which exists in the region. The hamlet of Algarabejo and a few other nearby villages are equally small, but Valdemora differs from all of them with the presence of the railroad settlement within its territorial limits. The feature of small size is not foreign to the region as a whole and necessitates no qualification of the terms in which units of the social structure regard one another. The railroad settlement, on the other hand, brings farmers into contact with people who have no place in the traditional system of classification of personal statuses. They are not forasteros to Valdemora, because they live within the village limits. But neither are they vecinos of the común or children of the pueblo. Their women are wives and casadas in the general sense, but not in the corporate sense, and hence the semantic confusion which Valdemorans, unlike their neighbors, fall into. The terms *de la RENFE, de afuera* (from outside), or *de abajo* refer to nonfarmers (some of whom are not

23. In parts of the northern peninsula, according to the Ateneo questionnaire (1901), brides are bidden formal farewells by the group of mozas. The questionnaire reports from Asturias that, when a girl marries a forastero, the mozos of her village do not attend the wedding; they are displaced by the fellow mozos of the groom.

with the railroad) and serve as modifiers for terms, such as mozo, which in other villages unequivocally refer to común members.

The presence of resident outsiders creates more than semantic complications. Some outsiders have technically become members of the común, and they create some difficulties in the traditional definition of its boundaries. Valdemorans unhesitatingly cite the requirements of común membership as I have described them here, and always active farming is one of them. But in recent history three nonfarmers have joined the común. All three were storekeepers or artisans, all three resided in the pueblo itself, and all three had either grown up in the vicinity or married into común families. The crucial factor in these cases appears to have been that all three families kept some livestock (either goats or mules) and thus needed pasture rights, and none of them, being self-employed, had unquestionable access to expropriated railroad lands. Living in the pueblo, these individuals cast their lot with their neighbors in the común, petitioning for membership, partaking of communal resources, and shouldering the concomitant obligations to attend council meetings and participate in cendera. One of these men is now dead; his son, who followed his example, has emigrated; and the third, the mason, has withdrawn from the común. This withdrawal came around the time the mason ceased to keep goats, but the immediate cause was an argument with the alcalde regarding the mason's contribution to communal labor. There are more than two sides to such a story, and several versions of the argument are current, but they share in common the fact that the sentimental basis of común membership failed to hold the mason when he felt that the demands on his time outweighed the benefits he received. As a nonfarmer, he felt the demands more heavily than others and at the same time had the means by which to survive without access to communal resources. He has, however, retained his membership in the burial society, which dates from his entrance into the común.

Aid to bereaved families is a service which, unlike such things as livestock insurance, need not necessarily be limited to farmers alone. All families in the pueblo are at times bereaved and seek to bury their dead in the cemetery. But the mason and his wife, a daughter of the pueblo, are the only nonfarmers who have joined the society. The other resident children of the pueblo are not members of the society, though they have kinsmen and sentimental ties in the pueblo and expect to die there. The burial society statutes require a double fee from nonmembers for maintenance of cemetery plots, but in practice nonmembers are charged no more than members. The community's bark is worse than its bite in its dealings with resident nonfarmers. There remains, thus, only one tangible benefit from burial society membership—that is that the adra is automatically activated for gravedigging when a member dies. But the disadvantage for nonmembers is again less than it would seem, since men always volunteer to help a bereaved nonmember family outside the context of the adra, and the outsiders remain without the obligation to reciprocate.

We are left, then, with the fact that the formal written statutes of the village's corporate organizations and people's own statements of the rules involve stipulations which are sometimes modified in practice: the común waives the question of active farming when an individual is willing to comply with the other obligations of membership, and the burial society effectively offers nonmembers the same benefits which go to members.

The question of común membership in marginal cases throws light on the economic aspects of the corporate organization. The marginal families—the three nonfarmers who joined or the part-time farmer who did not join—could not have lived in the village at all without recourse to what we might call "import" products: fuel other than the local wood, meat from sources other than the local flocks, and cash incomes with which to purchase all items they did not grow themselves. It was the size of their incomes and the availability of goods from outside which made their positions tenable in the twentieth century. The presence in Valdemora of the railroad and its workers, creating a greater market for services and more jobs, allows some people a greater choice of life-style. In

Valdemora it is possible for some to opt for or against corporate membership; this choice is not a real one in most neighboring towns. The mason kept goats for milk even while one of the stores sold cow's milk; in another town the mason might have had to maintain goats for the family's milk, but would have little chance in most other towns to support himself in his trade. Far from forcing us to change our view of what the común is, Valdemora's marginal cases serve to underline the fact that the común is essentially exactly what its charter and its members claim it to be—an organization of full-time farmers and herders. For farmers, the común is the focal center of deep-seated sentiment and religious tradition as well as of economic cooperation. The composition of the burial society is interesting not so much in that nonfarmers do not join, but in that all farmers do join: the burial society can be viewed as one face of the común's existence, its members bound by the same ties which bind them as común members and which distinguish them from the outsiders.

Although outsiders are seldom involved in corporate affairs and constitute a residual category in traditional terms, the small size of the común allows them, at times, to play important roles, but never in formal ceremonial contexts. Thus, whereas in many respects the mozos of the común must function as a very small group, for purposes of organizing dances and hiring bands for fiestas they have long cooperated with the mozos of the station barrio—neither group could bear the financial burden alone. Members of the farm community feel that the presence of the outsiders and of the railroad itself has made Valdemora more resistant to the depopulation and corporate breakdown which have affected the other very small villages in the region. Farmers attribute their común's remarkable cohesiveness directly to both the village's small size and the residence of outsiders within it, factors which have often been thought to destroy rural traditions.

# Family Estates

> We people are bad and we fight over things, so it's better that we stay apart and keep our things separate. Parents love their children, but children are always thinking "how much can I get?", so we make careful inventories and everything is clear.
>
> —A Valdemora vecino and father

Active farming defines membership in the corporate village, but most aspects of estate management and the transmission of lands fall outside the sphere of corporate action in Valdemora. The town council's formal concern with farming is limited to the regulation of the biennial rotation and the use of water for irrigation, since grain stubble and water are defined as communally held resources. The ownership of cultivated land is, on the other hand, entirely individual, and farmers are free to exploit it as they wish. The separation of farm land from the realm of communal holdings is marked in Valdemora, and the village in this sense represents something of an extreme among the traditionally corporate communities of the north. In some regions in recent history town councils closely regulated the use of farm lands, as in true open-field systems, or even held title to them and periodically effected their redistribution among member families.[1] In Valdemora there is a strong bias against any intrusion of communal administration into the realm of agriculture. This, then, is an area in which the household is the largest cooperating unit, mobilizing its own labor and administering its own property. Associations rarely cross

1. See, for example, data reported in Costa 1898; Costa 1902; Costa et al. 1902; Dias 1948, 1953.

household lines in agricultural activities, for these are not considered the appropriate arena for interaction among vecino families. The "horizontal" principle which groups members of the común together by common age and sex is inactive in the context of farming.

The diversified estate on whose produce a family subsists must provide food for the family and fodder for the stock. The extent to which a vecino is able to decide freely what to produce, within the limits recognized by tradition, depends partly upon the number and kinds of animals he wants or needs to keep. The gradual shift from cows to mules for draft in the last two centuries reduced the use of meadows but required increased cultivation of oats. A man who keeps a larger flock of sheep produces more fodder grains for winter feed. A family which decides to raise more pigs than usual devotes a greater proportion of its garden land to fodder-greens. Families appropriate their resources quite differently in many respects, but it is still possible to describe a list of produce which is common to all households: wheat, barley, oats, chick-peas, vetch, potatoes, and garden vegetables. The list of livestock is equally standard: sheep, mules, pigs, chickens, and occasionally doves and other fowl, and rabbits. Apiculture is traditional in the region and has recently been revived in Valdemora after a lapse of some years. It is clear from a variety of sources that the most rapid changes have occurred with respect to those products which are not part of the daily diet. For example, there has been a certain amount of experimentation with fodder-legumes, and vetch at present replaces others which were cultivated a few years ago, but chick-peas have long been the staple legume in the diet and no vecino thinks of eliminating them.

People resist any dependence on outside sources for what they consider their most basic staples. The diet has changed over the centuries, of course, but most informants are unable to see major changes in their lifetimes, although they are able to document noticeable change in other areas. Some farmers experiment more consistently than others and their successes may then be adopted by their neighbors. The spread of new information within the community creates general similarities in what people are doing, but there are leaders and followers with respect to the adoption of new practices. Still, no farmer to date has broken out of the limits of a diversified, subsistence-oriented, mixed farming economy. Valdemorans pride themselves on being able to supply their own tables and not on their success in market ventures. Although the latter are becoming more and more important, the era of the Civil War lives in people's minds as a recent reminder that things can go wrong at any time and, when they do, only the subsistence farmer is likely to have meat, vegetables, and bread on his table. This conviction is every bit as strong as the contradictory one that the farmer lives under the constant threat of famine from natural causes and it is sometimes safer to be salaried. These two notions of security underlie both the tenacity with which emigrants from Valdemora maintain their ties with the land and, simultaneously, the villagers' view of emigration as the only way to achieve financial independence from the forces of nature. Financial security is achieved primarily outside the village, while the psychological security of having a source of food is the Valdemoran's birthright.

Estate partibility and equal inheritance by all children form the basis for an egalitarian ideology which dominates Valdemora's social life. Customary law permits none of the freedom of disposition of portions of estates which is permitted under the Spanish civil code.[2]

Castilian law permits the free disposition of one-third of a person's inherited property; two-thirds (the *legítima*) must be transmitted to the legal heirs, but only one-half of this amount must be divided equally among the heirs. The other half may be granted to a favored heir or heirs, though the usufruct of this portion is reserved for a widowed spouse until his or her death. These provisions govern the disposition of both parents' inherited property only, and do not necessarily apply to the disposition of *ga-*

2. Código civil español 1966. Cf. bk. 3.

*nanciales*, the earnings accruing to the estate of either or both spouses during their marriage. The chief formal stipulation regarding joint earnings is that a widowed spouse acceeds to one-half of the total joint gains, but these need not be transmitted to the legal heirs at the time of the surviving parent's death.

By comparison with codified law, the local practice of transmitting equal amounts of all types of property to all children, of either sex, is uncompromising. Gananciales are transmitted according to the same rules which govern the parents' inherited estates. All property is destined to be divided into equal shares for all the heirs, with an interim arrangement providing for widowed spouses. If a man leaves a widow, a son, and a daughter, one-half of all his property goes to his widow. The other half is divided into equal parts—in this case three parts—to pass to his children and his widow. A widowed person always holds one-half of his spouse's estate, plus a fraction of the second half, in addition to his own inherited property. At his death, all of this is divided equally among the heirs. If a widow or widower remarries and has children in the second marriage, siblings and half-siblings inherit equal shares from their common parent's own property, but their fortunes may differ significantly with respect to the holdings of the other parent. The children of the first marriage have no rights in their step-parent's estate; the children of the second marriage cannot receive parts of that portion (one-half plus a fraction) of their parent's holding which proceeds from the death of his first spouse: that amount must be held in reserve for the heirs of the first marriage. In addition, the first and second marriages may have significantly different additional earnings, and the establishment of the different heirs' rights here may become problematic. It is in cases of second marriages which produce children that customary law is forced to deal with gananciales as a separate category—this is currently an issue in one Valdemora family (see chapter 4). Finally, the only instances in which an adjustment *(mejora)* is ever made in favor of a single heir is when a child is regarded as either physically or mentally disabled.

If this is the case, by either spoken or written word, one or both parents may leave him something extra to assure his permanent security. In Valdemora, a mejora never amounts to as great a proportion of a total estate as is permitted by national law; it usually consists of the dedication to the disabled child of one or two fields, yielding enough wheat in rent for yearly sustenance, or sometimes a house site, assuring permanent shelter. A mejora may also be a stipulation that the disabled person be cared for in some way agreed upon by his siblings—for instance, by his residing with them by turns.

Valdemorans recount the histories of individuals receiving mejoras to illustrate the local concern for providing for all people, regardless of their condition. Yet out of these stories grows a second—and more embarrassing—point: human avarice has led many relatives of favored heirs to mistreat them. Some families are said to have tried to hide the fact that a feeble-minded sibling indeed held land or a house in order that he might be institutionalized as a ward of the state at no cost to the family. Local lore contains several instances in which charity hospitals discover the truth about such wards and order their property officially confiscated in return for services rendered. The greedy siblings are not the only villains of such stories. Since state charity hospitals are administered by the Church, which is also viewed as avaricious, their personnel—usually the nuns—are pictured as swooping into the villages as vultures after prey, annexing village fields and houses as state property. This does not, in fact, happen often, and families are able to make the adjustment in cash once their debt is discovered. Further, as I shall discuss later, people never tell such stories about their fellow vecinos, but, rather, about other villagers or long-deceased members of the común. In general, arrangements to care for widowed or disabled persons by housing them or contributing to their support are viewed as a burden on sibling groups. There are frequent stories of failure of a sister or brother to contribute his proper share of a relative's support. In such instances, custom supports the exclusion of the delinquent from the division of the property of the disabled person, should the latter die. The delinquent's share is divided among the remaining siblings as compensation for the extra burden caused them.

Only one Valdemoran in memory has left a will. He was a farmer who had no children of his own, but whose wife had a son by a former marriage. The farmer willed to his stepson as much of his estate as was legally possible, and the remainder reverted to his own brothers. The stepson, now a vecino, gradually bought and rented enough shares from village emigrants to amass a full-scale holding.

In the more usual cases of intestate death, family members follow a standard procedure to divide movable and immovable property into the requisite number of equal lots. Farmers always possess documents regarding the size and land-quality of each of their fields. The heirs draw up lists of all fields with equal totals of area of each official land type. All of these calculations today are based on the cadastral survey figures and land-type classification of 1935, which has been kept up-to-date. Single fields are rarely divided; rather, there is an attempt to insure that all heirs receive equal amounts of each kind of land. (Cadastral documents show that there has been essentially no partition of single fields at least from the time of the 1750 survey of the Marqués de la Ensenada. This tradition long antedates the legislation prohibiting the partition of fields below a certain size.) Movable property is also divided into separate lots—all heirs decide together on the equivalence of different items as they are divided up. There is a livestock count, and lists of animals of various kinds and conditions are drawn up, again in the requisite number of equal lots.[3] Finally each list of fields is placed with a list of livestock and movables,

3. Complete property inventories drawn up in this context in the eighteenth and nineteenth centuries constitute an important series of documents preserved in the town archive. Such lists serve as bases for the assessment of inheritance taxes *(derechos reales)*, but they are no longer filed with the alcalde. The listing of current cash value of all goods makes these documents invaluable sources for economic historians.

and when everyone has agreed on the justice of the division, the heirs draw lots for their shares. This technique of assigning shares to their new owners is the same one described for the Greek village of Vasilika.[4]

The cash assets of the deceased are divided as is his property, after outstanding debts and funeral expenses have been paid. A nonfarmer, of course, accepts a cash equivalent for such things as livestock, which are maintained on the farmstead, but these transactions are made following the lottery. Many families own two house sites. One of these is often already occupied by a married child who is farming the estate. In such a case, nonresident heirs receive appropriate proportions of the cash value of the house sites. Sometimes, however, they may prefer shares in the actual ownership and collect rent from the heirs who already occupy the homes. By this arrangement, many emigrants from the farm community have potential living quarters in the village, and a few have insisted upon using them, at some inconvenience to their farmer-kinsmen. The psychological importance of the potential *pied à terre* is great, and some nonfarm families owe their comfortable existence in Valdemora to the fact that they do use such living quarters. People also (for example, Households 12, 14, and 15, table 2) often exploit small plots of inherited land, usually for vegetables only.

Occasionally the heirs to a man's estate, sometimes including his widow, choose to administer their inherited farm lands as a corporation. In these cases, title to all fields passes to *herederos de X* (heirs of X) and the active farmers pay rent to siblings on proportions of the holding, but without reference to specific fields. Only one estate is presently administered in this way.

Widowers, who are by definition already vecinos, always retain active control of their estates, including their portion of their deceased wives' holdings, even though they may be retired from active farming. Widows may choose the same course. In such

4. Friedl 1964; Levy 1956.

cases, the window or retired widower collects rent on the entire farm from the son who actively works it. Thus, many widows achieve full landlord status in cadasters. When the widowed parent dies, the heirs acquire title to the estate and the active farmer pays rent to his siblings on their shares. Widows, unlike widowers, sometimes relinquish title to estates upon their husbands' deaths. There is one such case currently, and others in recent memory. Here, the widow enters into a contract with her heirs, who bind themselves to contribute equally to her support, and she gives them title to their shares of the estate and thus cannot collect rent. She usually retains the use of a house, however. In one curious case of a widow considered mentally incompetent, her heirs agreed to give her the produce of a few plots plus a salary of five pesetas a day until her death. (The term *sueldo*, or salary, is used to describe these and similar arrangements among kinsmen.) She retained control of one house, shared with a bachelor son. Other families in town viewed this arrangement as the result of avarice, rather than common sense, and regarded it as crippling to the heirs' freedom, since the tiny salary forced their mother into a semidependent position and kept her a burden to them. Criticism is not of the nature of the arrangement, but simply of the small size of the salary.

The relationship between vecinos, either active or retired, and their adult children who also actively farm, whether married or single, is also a contractual one. Children always "work for the house." But a young man traditionally has the option to work for wages, near home or elsewhere, and his decision to stay on the farm is at this point regarded as an occupational decision. His parents begin to pay him a salary as if he were a hired assistant, thus making him financially independent. The arrangement probably takes effect after the age of seventeen, but I am uncertain of some details, because families do not like to discuss contracts between members of the household. They consider such arrangements necessary, but somehow not ideal characteristics of parent-child relations. When the farmer-son lives in his parents' household, his salary is adjusted so that, in effect, he is paying his parents for room and board. The situation is the same whether or not the father is largely retired, as long as the son is single. The father, if he is not too old, may cease farming and devote most of his time to watching sheep. The families who keep sheep today are those with either two generations of active males or several younger males who have not yet emigrated. If a man stays in the village in order to tend his family's sheep, he too is salaried by his kinsmen, as is a young farmer. If the son is married, he represents a separate household, probably occupying the second house owned by his family, and he is feeding his own family. Thus, he pays rent to his father on all he works, but gains effective control of the farming operation. It is he, as farmer, who begins to make investments in machinery, to experiment with new produce, and so on. A son's marriage and entrance into the común tend to signal at least semiretirement for his father from both herding and farming.

A salaried son, unlike an unrelated hired man, is expected to lend a hand in household chores without thinking always of recompense. At present, no one in town fails notably in this respect. But the notion that even an older and salaried son owes his family a debt extends also to those who emigrate to work outside the village, although distance lessens the parental controls in these cases. There are oft-cited cases of sons who earned good wages in factory jobs in large cities and did not send money home. This failure is taken into account when a son's marriage preparations are made.

Part of the marriage preparation for women involves the gathering of the trousseau *(ajuar)*—mostly household linens and some clothing, all embroidered by the women of her family; and some household equipment and furniture, always including the bed. Men may or may not receive from their parents an equivalent type of gift, consisting minimally of a new suit for the wedding. In the cases mentioned above where men did not share their wages with their families, they usually receive nothing at marriage, except that the groom's parents always pay an amount of the wedding expenses proportional to the number of guests from their side. Girls, on the other hand, do not leave home as often as their brothers. They continue to "work for the house" even as mozas, yet they generally receive no salary. The trousseau, which usually represents a large investment, appears to replace a salary; it is amassed during exactly the same years in which a man would be salaried. In addition, on almost every afternoon during all these years, a girl passes a few hours embroidering her linens. If a girl leaves home to take a job—not a new practice, since girls have long been sent into domestic service[5]—she almost always sends a large part of her wages home. A good and proper girl, whose room and board are arranged and her social life closely chaperoned, does not have much to spend money on. Thus, whether they leave home or not, girls are usually considered to have "worked for the house." No girl is ever denied her trousseau. It is interesting that there is not even a name for the gift to men. People sometimes use the word *hijuela,* but this term is variously applied to all heritable goods and to inventories thereof, and for unequivocal reference to the bridegroom's gift people have to resort to calling it "the suit and things."

The fact that parents consider some children more deserving of wedding gifts contrasts with the egalitarian ideals stated on the subject. People say that the trousseaus of all daughters should be equal and that, though sons' gifts are always smaller, they should be equal for all sons, and that records should be kept. These records play a potential role in later estate division, when it becomes clear that some children have received less from their parents than have other siblings of the same sex. In practice, people

5. This is less common today than a generation ago, when elder daughters of families with many children were sent to serve families in nearby larger towns. Their younger sisters grew up in less crowded circumstances and usually "worked for the house." Today, families are smaller and most girls stay at home until they are married.

avoid recording gifts to their children precisely because all the gifts are not equal. It is in this area that people escape from the pressures of open record-keeping and the demands of giving equal treatment. It is interesting that the major investment at stake, the trousseau, is given in fairly close accord with the ideal, just as salaries are. The departure from the ideal in the case of the bridegroom's gift is sometimes chiefly a symbolic departure, for the gift may represent only a minor real investment. On the other hand, the price of a man's suit, not to mention a whole trousseau, is not necessarily negligible in the farmer's terms. The investment at the time of the wedding may be the last material aid a child receives from his parents during their lifetime, for parents are not usually able to help a young couple in any significant way. Thus, the imbalances which may exist in the parents' gifts to their children arise out of the only context in which tradition allows them to act on the recognition that their children, as people, have not behaved identically toward their parents. Otherwise, with respect to the transmission of material goods, tradition requires the identical treatment of all heirs.

A couple's marriage necessitates an economic adjustment in each family, and it was formerly the custom for the newlyweds either to remain with their respective families or to co-reside with one set of parents until the first harvest after their marriage. Separate residence is most frequently stated as the ideal, and this accompanied the ideal cases of endogamous matches. Only older informants attest to these practices, and the younger generation is horrified to learn of them: co-residence with elders is avoided today and separation of the spouses is unheard of. The apparent reason for such arrangements was that the young couple could not farm independently until they had their own seed to sow, and people could only lay claim to such a proportion of their parents' harvest after they were married (rather than simply engaged) and after having worked for the house(s) as married people for a full season. The widow Josefa, speaking of her older sister, describes the arrangement of the turn of the century:

> She was still with my mother, and he with his father; they hadn't gone to their house yet. They still weren't living together. He would go there to sleep [with her] and each of them was working with his own father. While they're sowing the wheat your parents maintain you for a year until they harvest the wheat and have everything ready and then you go to your own house. I didn't do that because my husband [her sister's widower] already had his own planted from the time he'd first married. My brother was also in my father's house until he harvested—he and his wife were both with my mother. They can't go 'til they bring in the harvest; it's not like people who have a salary. My other sister, who also married a farmer, went to Aguasalida and stayed with his parents for a year—until the harvest. . . . My son and his wife did the same thing: she came here to sleep but later went home to eat.

This was a parent-child contract analogous to that of a salaried mozo with his father: here a year's labor, of one or both new spouses in a parental household, was exchanged for a portion of the harvest or other goods which, when the period ended, effected the formation of the new economic unit which the marriage ceremony alone could not create.

It was ideal that both parental families contribute equally to the establishment of the new household, but this required the separation of the new spouses. The ideal was best achieved by couples from the same village, but some cases of separate residence in neighboring villages have been cited to me as well. The respective needs of the two parental households were also taken into consideration. A norm or ideal, or both, of one year's separate dwelling has been documented elsewhere in Spain,[6] but not recently. Valdemorans cannot offer specific reasons for the disappearance of former residence practices, but modern expressions of distaste for them indicate that the gradual increase in the farmer's cash surplus and reduced needs for large labor forces have allowed people to choose a way which they find preferable. Although newlyweds now always live together, and usually alone together, the arrangement between a father and his newlywed

6. Particularly in the northwest; cf. Ateneo 1901.

farmer-son still follows the traditional pattern. Even though the new couple may reside in its own quarters, the son still works with his father until after the first year's harvest, receiving seed as at least part of his salary for that year. Only after the harvest does the couple become financially independent. The continuance of this tradition became evident at the marriage of a young farmer in 1967.

Estates are worked by nuclear-family households. Thus farm operations are always under the direction of a vecino, whether he holds title to lands or pays rent to a parent. An unmarried farmer and his father work a farm cooperatively, but a married farmer and his father keep their households' affairs as separate as possible. At least today, they do not form a two-generation labor force for combined farming and herding; these activities are considered part of a single household's enterprise and no nuclear-family head—not even a retired vecino—devotes his full time to herding if he is not also actively directing a farm, rather than simply collecting rents from a son's household.

The dispersion throughout the municipality of the many fields constituting any single estate has profound effects on the way agricultural activities are organized. The lands of the municipality fall into irregular *parajes*—areas of contiguous fields—which bear traditional names. These parajes are ecological units most often of a single land class. Contiguous areas which are used differently or are of significantly different quality tend to be distinguished by name as well—for example, within the paraje called *la Sierra,* the *hoya* (hollow) *de la Sierra* and *majadas* (corrals) *de la Sierra* are distinguished; similarly, *la Cabezota* contains the *hoya de la Cabezota, suertes* (bounded plots) *de la Cabezota, alto* (high part) *de la Cabezota,* and so on. The Valdemora survey of 1935 (map 3) shows the layout of the fields in relation to the habitation center. The large, undifferentiated areas on the map are generally the hilltops and steeper slopes, uncultivated pasture and woodland, communally used and held by the House of Medinaceli.

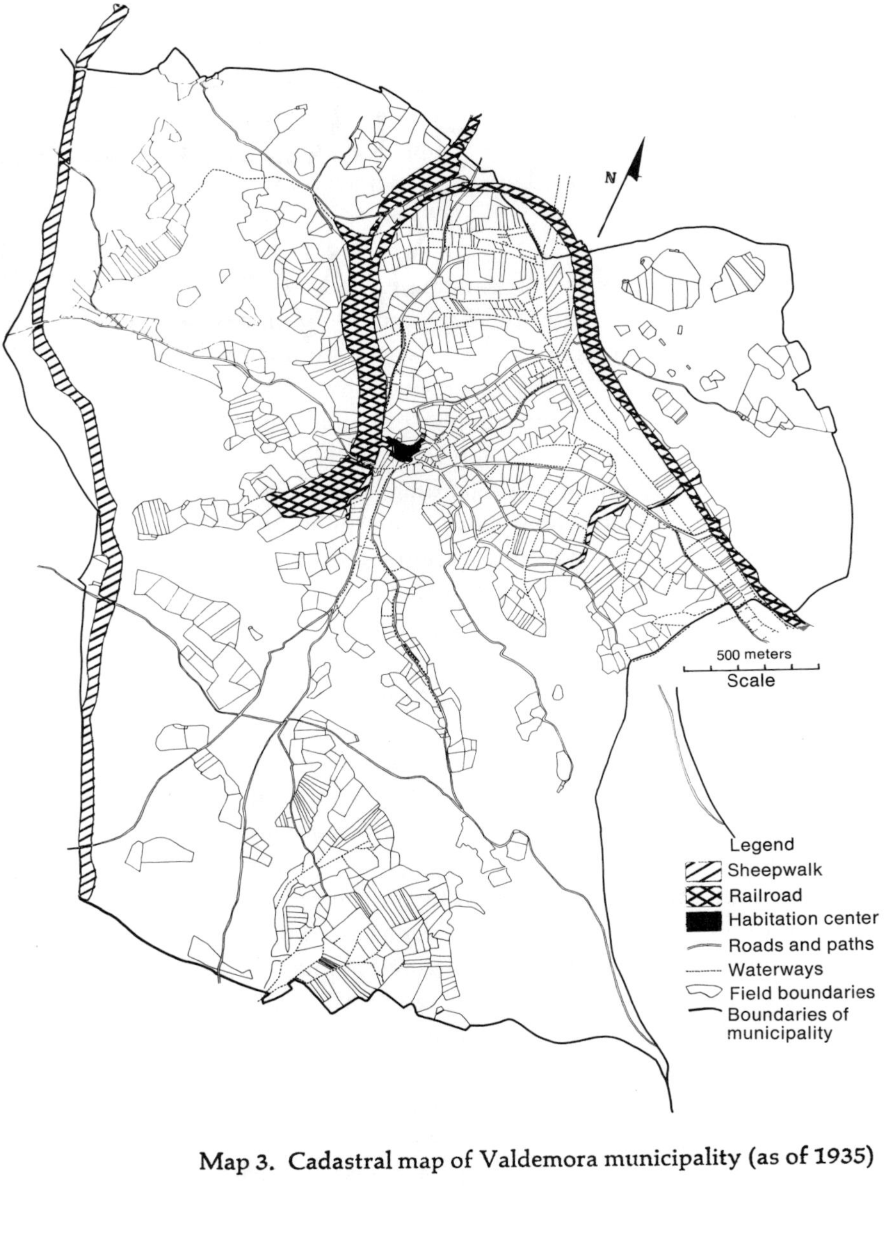


Map 3. Cadastral map of Valdemora municipality (as of 1935)

1. The plaza as seen from the Castillo

2. Facing the Castillo

3. Entering the plaza on the road from the station and church

4. A closer view of the fountain and lavadero

5. Mule-drawn plows (*left*, Roman plow; *right*, rotating mold-board plow)

6. Plowing the fallow for planting

7. A man harvests with scythe while his wife follows, gleaning

8. The flint-toothed threshing sledge, or trillo

9. Riding the trillo on the threshing floor (1963)

10. Valdemora's first tractor draws the trillo (1963).

11. Machine winnowing and the bagging of grain (1963)

12. The communal thresher-winnower at work (1966)

13. A shepherd grazes his sheep above newly plowed fields

14. Men carry San Antonio in procession

15. Morning shopping

16. Washing at the lavadero

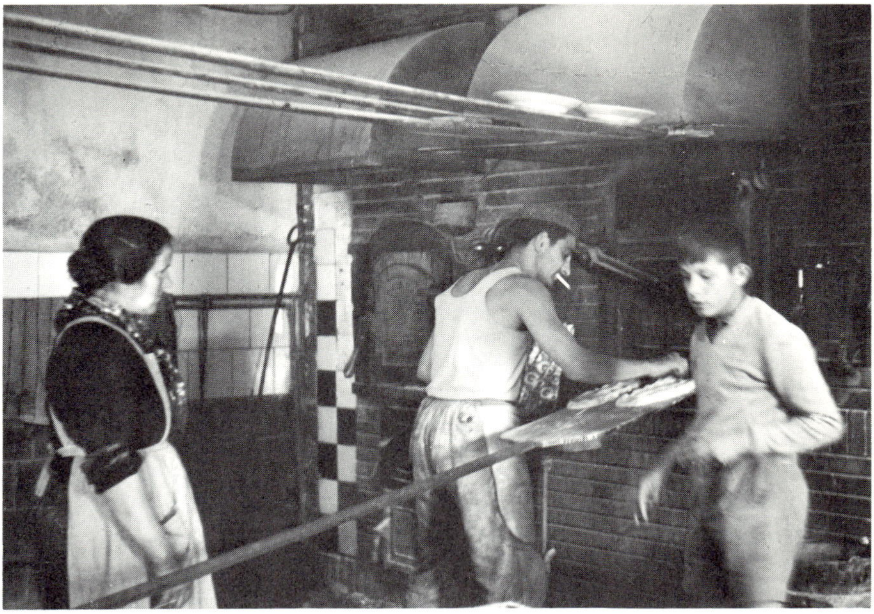

17. Using the bakery oven for fiesta baking

18. The Sunday afternoon card game

19. Women carry San Antonio in procession

20. Decorated cakes and fruit to hang on the bough

21. The mozos prepare to decorate the oak bough for the fiesta of San Isidro.

22. The mozos lead the procession of the saint

23. The mozas (and onlookers) prepare to decorate the plaza for the fiesta of San Isidro.

24. Mozas take their turn carrying San Antonio

25. Girls and boys take opposite places at the head of a procession, just behind the mozas (not shown).

26. The girls pose for a photograph

An estate may consist of nearly 100, or more, separate fields, approximately half of which are cultivated yearly. There is today only one tract of land in the municipality that is irrigated, and there every family has plots of garden land. Cereal lands are scattered on all sides of the village, and all families have holdings of every land class—from first to sixth class cereal land—on the more gentle slopes and in the valley. No two parajes are worked by the same group of owners; a man's field-neighbors differ in every sector and for every field. Other types of property are also scattered in the same fashion. Each estate includes a threshing floor *(era)*—a high, flat plot exposed to the wind—on the periphery of the settlement. (Some villages in the region have a single, communally owned threshing floor, but even then threshing is not usually a cooperative activity.) The only structures which are located outside the village nucleus are sheep corrals *(parideras)*, on hillside plots, used especially in the lambing season. A family may have one or more of these in different pasture areas located along the hillside grazing routes. The flocks are sometimes left there while the shepherd returns briefly to the village. In addition, every family has, in the habitation center itself, the following properties: a pig-sty *(corte)*, a chicken house *(gallinero)*, at least one storage barn *(pajar)* for grain and fodder storage, and a mule stable *(cuadra)*, which generally adjoins the family's house or comprises its ground floor. Structures other than the mule stable are scattered throughout the village without reference to the house site. Beehives are kept on any family plot which is favorable for honey production.

Any villager, in the performance of his routine tasks, must move separately from his neighbors, though their paths may often cross. This situation in itself would make difficult any consistent cooperation across household lines for work on individually owned properties. But the difficulty is intensified by the sentimental aspects of personal ownership, for each field is more than a plot of land; it is a piece of family history, literally—from the moment of estate division—a farmer's lot in life by virtue of his family membership. Fields, barns, and houses are parts of a family's identity: marked boundaries separate them on all sides from sites which represent different families. Adults and children alike know who owns and works each field in town; people locate fields verbally with reference to their shape, surrounding landmarks, and other owners in the paraje; children punctuate their excursions through the local scenery with identifications of their own family holdings, referring to fields, trees, and houses as "mine." The physical aspects of the land tenure system have slowed the mechanization of farming in the region, but the psychological and sentimental concomitants of the traditional land tenure system have been the major factors in Valdemora's rejection of land reform programs (see chapter 6).

The produce of farms is processed, disposed of, and consumed by nuclear-family households. There is neither corporate coordination nor consistent spontaneous cooperation in these affairs. The problem of spoilage which besets families in questions of mutton consumption hardly exists with respect to other farm produce of the traditional economy. Grain, honey, and pork products are preserved; eggs and milk are consumed in small, regular quantities; poultry is rapidly consumed, and vegetables are either eaten in season or canned. The traditions surrounding meat sharing described in chapter 2 and to be reexamined in the next chapter are the only traditions of food sharing. In no sense does any other produce circulate between the households, and the traditional feasts of the whole village are the only occasions on which members of different kin groups eat together.

The farmer maintains complete control of the manner of disposition of anything which is not used at home; for goods and services he patronizes whom he pleases. No two families patronize all of the same merchants, in or out of Valdemora. Artisans and specialists of various kinds are traditionally dispersed throughout the Sierra Ministra. Within easy range by mule from Valdemora, scattered through the small villages, are three flour mills, at least two fodder mills, two wool weavers, several general stores and blacksmiths, and so on. Such facilities are all duplicated in Sigüenza, but villagers in the Valdemora area tend to use Sigüenza primarily for items of clothing, household equipment, and specialty foods. People do not necessarily patronize the closest localities and they are not deterred by distance; the tradition of travel is also closely associated with the dispersion of kinsmen throughout the region. Families systematically exchange some goods and services with certain of their kinsmen in other farm communities. For example, relatives east of the Sierra sometimes send beans, which are more commonly grown there, in exchange for chick-peas. Farmers from wine and orchard country to the east sometimes exchange their products for hams, which people feel are best cured at higher altitudes. But, once again, Valdemorans do not depend on these exchanges for what they consider staples. The railroad serves as a vehicle for many such exchanges. In addition, the railroad gives people access to goods and services in places where they do not necessarily have kinsmen or previous familiarity.

In short, families act as independent units in forming economic contracts with whomever they please. Networks of exchange are far-flung: they are bound neither by corporate action nor by the territorial boundaries of the village. We are describing what is, in effect, a residual category of activities in which farmers' village membership is neither a binding nor a crucial factor. This whole sphere of activities, which is very large, is dominated by behavioral ideals which support the individual's freedom to run his own life without permitting him to escape from the constraints of corporate membership. People do not openly involve themselves in each other's private affairs, but the community at large has on call enough *sub rosa* information about everybody's activities that individuals can be kept in line in questions of major concern. People believe that outstanding debts, social or financial, can ruin the social harmony upon which the corporate común depends. Careful itemization of accounts, sharp definition of property boundaries, tendencies not to cooperate except under carefully contracted arrangements, and fierce protection of private independence are all viewed as essential for the maintenance of community on the corporate level.

# The Maintenance of Order

4

I don't think it makes any difference what god a person believes in. What's important is that we stand in awe of something.

—A vecino

Mere description of the corporate activities of the común is not sufficient explanation of the binding nature of membership and the sentimental basis of the común's continuity. What the común does formally does not tell us fully what the común is. The less obvious, but most important aspects of its existence can be approached through the analysis of social control in the village. What might seem to be the primary machinery of control—the explicitly political and judicial faces of the community—are in reality only secondary forces in village life; a review of these aspects of village organization is instructive in showing us that we must turn elsewhere with the bulk of our questions.

An ayuntamiento is the smallest seat of government within a provincial judicial district *(partido judicial)*. An ayuntamiento, however, can encompass more than a single municipality, which is in this area the basic unit of territorial organization and the focus of sentiment.[1] The merging of municipalities under a single

1. In parts of Spain with more diverse settlement pattern (in most of the north, for example), municipalities may contain a variety of subunits which may or may not be nucleated. Nomenclature varies from region to region; municipalities may contain some or all of the units called *villa, lugar, aldea, barrio,* or *caserío,* and an ayuntamiento may serve many municipalities. The provincial volumes of the census,

ayuntamiento is a fact of long standing but, in the Sierra Ministra at least, appears to be largely arbitrary. Today, ayuntamientos themselves are being merged to provide greater effciency in local government. The Valdemora and Algarabejo municipalities have "depended upon" the ayuntamiento at Aguasalida at least since the establishment of provincial boundaries—that is, for almost a century and a half. This dependency, by definition, classifies Valdemora and Algarabejo as hamlets (aldeas) of Aguasalida. Municipalities below a certain population were in 1750 placed in a category of *despoblados* or very small settlements. If this word was intended to imply ongoing depopulation, the implication in the Sierra Ministra was largely false. A village like Valdemora had as large a population in 1750 as it had had since 1500 (the period of earliest available documentation), and Valdemora's size was still unchanged in the mid-twentieth century. Similar stability can be documented for many other Sierra villages which were called despoblados in the 1750 cadaster.

By virtue of its status as a hamlet, the alcalde of Valdemora is an *alcalde pedáneo.* He is responsible for collecting municipal taxes (*arbítrios*—taxes on animal property and on vehicles), but this income is received in and administered from Aguasalida. Aguasalida is the local seat of the judiciary as well, and any Valdemora disputes or disciplinary action taken by the alcalde must be processed there. National taxes are paid in Aguasalida when the collector announces the dates of his visits there.

The ayuntamiento of Aguasalida, after an informal review of possible candidates for alcalde pedáneo of a hamlet, nominates an individual, who is then officially named by the provincial governor. In order either to refuse nomination or to resign the post of alcalde, a man must state cause. The post carries no salary and little prestige and is looked upon as a burden. The vecinos handle

---

showing the breakdown of territorial units with separate identities, provide a good general guide to settlement pattern and relative size of population units; the general volumes of the census do not, since they deal with municipalities alone.

it as they handle other burdens, assuming it by turn. Most of the present vecinos have served in the office for a few years (the term is of indefinite length), eventually submitting their resignations, and the office has become in practice a rotating one. The alcalde's two assistants, the vice-alcalde (teniente) and the "third" (tercero)[2] are selected in the same way, but tend to remain longer in office as the burdens of their jobs are fewer. The aide (alguacil), as mentioned earlier, is the vecino most recently entered into the común unless, as occurred in 1966, that vecino becomes alcalde. In that instance, another vecino willingly assumed the office of alguacil, which was soon destined for a farmer about to marry and enter the común.

The Aguasalida ayuntamiento is composed of the same officials mentioned above plus three representatives from its two hamlets combined and a justice of the peace *(juez de paz)* with an assistant. Several ayuntamientos are served by a single secretary, an official trained for the post, who is the civil recorder.

Valdemora's officialdom, of course, represents both the railroad community and the pueblo. It is always the vecinos of the común, however, who fill offices. This is not a formal regulation, but is due rather to the farmers' greater commitment to the community and to tradition. It is also traditional that the alcalde, the teniente, and the tercero act in certain contexts as officials of the council of the común as well—for example, in organizing the livestock count preceding the payment of pasture rental, in handling details of other común accounts, and so on. These three men, and sometimes the alguacil, meet frequently; the men of the común meet with them as already described; but the entire constituency of the hamlet almost never meets. On only one recent occasion have the vecinos of civil status met with the vecinos of the común on an issue of common concern: this was with reference to the establishment of lunchroom service in the school.

It is the alcalde's responsibility to handle affairs forwarded to

2. This term once designated the official charged with collecting tithes and turning them over to the proper authorities.

him from Aguasalida or higher levels of the provincial government. It also falls to him to hear complaints on the local level and see that items of local business are carried to the proper places. Disputes and criminal offenses are to be brought first to his attention. The alcalde must notify the local unit of the Civil Guard (in Medinaceli) of any form of criminal action taking place in the municipality. He himself has power to place fines on parties in disputes—a first offense is fined at fifty pesetas, a second at one hundred pesetas, and a third may be set at the alcalde's discretion up to five thousand pesetas. But the alcalde himself must travel to Aguasalida in order to levy fines. No matter: no alcalde of Valdemora has placed a fine within living memory. Indeed, people's knowledge of the judicial process is limited to hearsay, for they have never activated it, and when questioned on the resolution of disputes, any Valdemoran answers: "Here we don't have disputes."

Indeed, there are no disputes. Altercations are classed as arguments *(discusiones)*, as quarrels *(peleas)*, or as disputes *(disputas)*. There are many arguments; but quarrels are serious breaches or ongoing hostilities, and typically the only events classed as quarrels are lovers' quarrels or incidents within single families. Disputes, which are formal almost by definition, have never grown out of these. Vecinos do not dispute (or quarrel), people say, "because we have to live together, and anyway we're all really like one family." The notion of the común as a family will be examined later; let us first examine the felt need for coexistence.

It is both futile and irrelevant to ask why human and natural resources are mobilized as they are in Valdemora rather than in some other way. It is a cultural fact that life in the village binds its members in certain ways and patterns their relationships to one another and to their personal and joint properties. Alternatives to some of these patterns are generally recognized, but the patterns are nonetheless perpetuated and manipulated only within limits. For example, the physical arrangement of the pueblo is such that even houses which are shielded from the general view at the edges of the nucleus are still within hearing distance, and there is no house which is not within sight of at least two others. There is some tendency to insulate houses by building the stables or a storage room on one side, so that the living quarters are not adjacent, and the many common walls are very thick. However, houses open directly onto the streets, as do their windows, and there is no such thing as a wall or fence shielding houses from the streets. Family gatherings, radio programs, and arguments can be heard outside. Villagers continually tread the thin line between overhearing and eavesdropping, between seeing and spying; they do not have to go far out of their way to keep abreast of their neighbors' affairs. Enough information flows through the community in the course of daily life that men, women, and children form an ever-present constabulary which awakens to unusually loud noises.

The centripetal tendency notable in the clustering of the dwellings is further heightened by the patterns of water use. Although there are private sources of water in town (several families have wells on their property), the only water which is exploited for human consumption (drinking and cooking) and for laundering is the communally owned public fountain (that is, the masonry construction catching spring water) and the public lavadero adjacent to it.[3] The unexceptioned dependence upon the fountain for all basic water needs brings people into public space and public view several times each day. Women wash at the lavadero and dry

3. I have reviewed the social patterns of water use with Professor Karl Butzer of the University of Chicago, a geomorphologist who has worked in the Sierra Ministra and in Valdemora itself. The geological data on the various water sources in town support the conclusion that the preferred fountain water is not different from water from some of the other sources in town, though these themselves vary. Dependence on the fountain is for primarily cultural, rather than physical, reasons; this is immediately evident when water use in the pueblo is compared with the different patterns which characterize the station barrio and the change in attitude of pueblo natives who move out of the social context of común membership. These matters are under separate study.

their laundry on the grass above it, in addition to making several daily trips to the fountain for household water. Every farmer passes the fountain on his way to and from the fields, morning, noon, and night, to water his animals.

There is strong resistance to any alteration of the patterns of water use, even by families who have wells (from which only the small stock are watered), and a variety of circular arguments are employed in support of the present system, though the women in particular suffer from the cold at the lavadero in winter. (Recently the availability of rubber gloves on the market has bolstered their morale.) As a result of the dependence on fountain water, the crossroad at one end of the cluster of houses where the fountain and lavadero are located is the most important physical locus of continual interaction across household lines. Here, in public and in view of many of the houses, the villagers meet in a casual context, feeding the grapevine while they harvest its fruits. It is interesting that the public water supply, represented especially by the fountain, is the chief symbol of village identity in the Sierra Ministra, and the church and saints are negligible in this respect.

The most prolonged public interaction occurs between the women in their hours at the lavadero. The lavadero functions as an observation center, and the women function as a clearing-house for general and public (not personal) gossip. The lavadero is the setting for that kind of gossip which serves to keep people within bounds; manipulative information exchange does not generally occur in this context, for people cannot select their associates in public places.[4] Custom strongly prohibits the expression of personal interest in those communally held areas to which everyone has access. Thus, we see separated on the physical scene the distinct social contexts which are marked by different behavioral

4. A view of the role of gossip in maintaining community cohesion (Gluckman 1963) is quite consonant with the view that gossip can also serve personal ends within a community (Paine 1967). The former kind of gossip is much more limited in the range of its content and its exchange is confined in Valdemora to specific settings and contexts.

constraints. In the public places whose administration is governed by the corporate charter, people's interaction, too, must conform to the ideals of equality, cooperation, and harmonious coexistence on which the charter is based. Activities in this sphere are destined to have a levelling effect.

Behavior in the private sphere, which is physically represented by private fields and houses, is marked by an ideal of family and individual autonomy. Inside the territorial limits of the village, families maintain autonomy in the administration of their internal affairs and in the disposal of their farm produce, and in doing so they also cross the territorial boundaries and enter into many kinds of relationships with outsiders. Indeed, in this realm people generally avoid their neighbors and the major traffic is between members of the same household and between Valdemorans and outsiders. The realm of the "dyadic contract" described by Foster[5] largely coincides in this case with that residual category of relationships which Barnes calls the "network," lying outside of both the territorial entity and corporate economic groups.[6] Obviously, there are constraints in this area, for the individual lives in two worlds. A person's freedom to create and manipulate his own image is hampered by his omnipresent neighbors, by their tendency to commit him to an image supported by accumulated public information about him, and by their power as a group to make of him an outcast.[7] These factors help to militate against quarreling within families as well as between vecinos, for such affairs always become known and color family reputations.

Although Valdemorans first proffer a definition of the común in economic terms, the power of the común over its members is hardly to be understood in those terms alone. "We have to live together" does not refer only to economic interdependence or to physical proximity, for these things are not necessarily contingent

5. Foster 1961, 1963.

6. Barnes 1954.

7. Aspects of this problem are much more thoroughly considered by the authors of *Honour and Shame* (Peristiany 1966) and by Gearing (1967).

upon each other. "We have to live together" means that people's lives are bound together in some more total sense. Patterns of housing and water use serve to maintain physical proximity and tight controls on a population which is bound by deeper imperatives to perpetuate such patterns. The común is at base a religious community as well as an economic one, spiritually as well as territorially bounded. The existence of a formal judiciary and the physical arrangement of the village can assure at best a modicum of cohesion; it is religious sanctions which support the quest for solidarity beyond mere cohesion and provide the imperatives which make the corporate charter a binding one.

An examination of Valdemora's ritual calendar shows a marked association of ritual events with collective activities in the común —that is, activities in which común members interact across household lines.[8] Valdemorans recognize three kinds of events which they regard as fiestas, and it should be emphasized that a fiesta per se is not necessarily associated with Catholic religious ritual. The use of the term *fiesta* in Valdemora is almost perfectly interchangeable with the English *feast* as "an elaborate meal often accompanied by a ceremony or entertainment,"[9] for all three kinds of fiesta have commensal aspects, and gatherings of kin or community which do not involve food sharing are not called fiestas at all (funerals dominate this category).

Family or private fiestas, *fiestas familiares,* occur on the few occasions regarded as festal which are not celebrated by all households simultaneously. These include the life-cycle events of baptism, first communion, and marriage;[10] and the occasions of the

8. A more detailed study of this association (Freeman 1968b) is in part summarized here.

9. The first meaning of *feast,* given in Webster's Third New International Dictionary.

10. Confirmation is not among these, and its celebration is confined to the hour of the mass alone. The bishop confirms villagers in groups at irregular intervals, often several years apart. Forty-year-olds may be confirmed along with six-year-olds who are still preparing for their first communion. Valdemorans regard confirmation as something of a technical formality.

sheep shearing and the pig slaughter. The distinctive feature of these occasions is that the food sharing which classes them as fiestas, although it is not confined to the nuclear family, unites people on the basis of kinship and friendship (crossing village lines), but never on the basis of común membership. Of the five events mentioned, baptism, first communion, and marriage are regarded as partially religious in nature because they specifically involve Catholic ritual; church attendance on these occasions does not normally involve the entire común, though first communions are an exception, as will be noted later. The shearing and the pig slaughter are not sanctified in any way and are regarded as entirely secular fiestas. Baptisms and weddings (and in one sense first communions) have some communal aspects which will be noted presently, but village-wide food sharing on these occasions is at best symbolic. Funerals are most similar to weddings in that they unite kin and friends in the same way, are observed in the church, and have communal aspects of similar type. The solemnity of funerals and the absence of food sharing by definition place them outside of the category of fiestas, although their magnitude suggests that we might simply call them "anti-fiestas," equivalent in a sense to fast days, where mourning dictates the abstention from those things which would mark any other event of comparable social scale and significance.[11]

Some kinds of family events consistently fall outside the category of fiestas. There is no kind of occasion on which the members of a single nuclear family may be said to celebrate a fiesta familiar. A family fiesta, by definition, involves kinsmen and friends from more than a single household and occurs with reference to the special events mentioned. Idiosyncratic and spontaneous celebrations are called *reuniones* (gatherings), or *juergas* (good times) and a variety of other slang names, such as the Ma-

11. The opposition of mourning-fasting to festal-commensal events which distinguishes funeral observance in Valdemora appears not to pertain, or to be less clear-cut, in areas of northwestern Spain where funeral wakes with full-scale banquets accompany mourning (cf. Ateneo 1901; Foster 1960). Wakes are called by special terms, however, and are always distinguished from fiestas.

drid slang terms *piripi or piripipí.* Into this category fall such events as birthdays, which are celebrated instead of saints' days and thus have no Catholic context. Before marriage, birthdays are also celebrated among female age-mates, but the event is regarded as minor.

Fiestas which involve the común as a body are classified either as ordinary fiestas, *fiestas corrientes,* or as fiestas which are recognized as special in some way, sometimes called *fiestas del pueblo.* This distinction is based on the presence or absence or specific events of food sharing involving the común as a whole or, secondarily, its corporate subgroups. Otherwise, both types are characterized by observance of the mass, attended by the entire común (in distinction to the masses accompanying family fiestas), and by relaxation from the daily routine. Although both types of fiesta may involve special foods, only the pueblo fiestas bring together non-kin to share special food in official and public space. On an ordinary fiesta, no matter what other activities engage the común members, families eat separately in their homes, and they have guests of their choosing. On pueblo fiestas, members of the común households eat prescribed foods together in prescribed places, and outsiders—including resident outsiders—are excluded from the proceedings.

Ordinary fiestas include all of the national holidays, such as Santiago, the national patron saint's day on 25 July, the Hispanization of America on 12 October, National Day (the Rising against the Republic) on 18 July, the Immaculate Conception on 8 December, and so on. All of these have some religious dimensions if they are not Catholic holidays per se. Businesses are closed, farmers are supposed not to work in the fields, and many city-dwellers visit friends and family in the village. Major fiestas of the Catholic cycle are also national fiestas, such as Corpus Christi, Easter, Christmas, New Year's Day, and Epiphany, in addition to those mentioned above. In the villagers' typology of events these are classed with "ordinary Sundays." They are days of general attendance at mass, of general relaxation, sometimes of visiting with kin from elsewhere, but not of communal feasting. In culinary terms, all ordinary fiestas are distinguished by family meals which differ from the daily fare, particularly in the inclusion of a first course of rice (a *paella*) and more than the ordinary amount of meat, poultry, or fish—most often poultry. Women describe ordinary fiesta meals as "just like Sundays," though a few special foods are associated with both Holy Week (including Easter) and the week of Christmas and New Year.

Two fiestas are celebrated locally with more than the usual fanfare, though in culinary terms they are still "ordinary." They are San Isidro (15–16 May), the feast of the village patron, and La Cruz de Septiembre (The Cross of September) or the Day of Our Lord (14–15 September, called "the September fiesta"), which honors the crucifix in the church. Both of these feasts have processional masses, like some of the pueblo fiestas and unlike all other ordinary fiestas except Corpus Christi (which also honors the church's crucifix). Both last for two days and have counterparts in every other nearby village,[12] most of which celebrate one major fiesta at the beginning of the crucial harvest season and one after it. Thus, the harvest is bracketed by a great deal of socializing across village lines, and numerous emigrants and absentees return to their villages of origin from urban areas and from other villages. No neighboring villages coincide in the celebration of the same major fiestas, for the success of their fiestas depends upon the attendance of all their neighbors.

Pueblo fiestas involve the común as a commensal unit. Chief among these today are San Antonio, on 13 June, and San Roque, on 16 August. On San Antonio, when pasturage accounts are drawn up, the men of the council slaughter and eat a lamb, using the house of the teniente alcalde. On San Roque, men of the común concoct a *sopeta*, a sweetened red wine in which bread is soaked. They consume this together in the meetinghouse, while their wives

12. Actually, of course, this pattern is general throughout rural Spain and in some urban centers as well.

are given a large supply to consume and distribute among the younger generation in the plaza. The feast had broader dimensions in the days of the distribution of the "Charity of San Roque." In chapter 2, I listed a number of occasions on which the subgroups of the común play roles: the chocolate brewing on San Juan; the confection of honey gachas on Todos los Santos; the merienda on Jueves Lardero; the suppers of vecinos and mozos on Shrove Tuesday after cendera; the mozos' merienda on the eve of Easter Sunday. All of these commensal events are defined in terms of the Catholic calendar. None of them involves the entire común in the celebration of mass, and the daily mass (which is featured only in villages with resident priests) presents no special features and attracts no more people than on other week days. The tendency to regard these as fiesta occasions despite the lack of fiesta-like observance of the mass indicates the importance of commensality in elevating events to the level of fiestas. There is, in other words, a tendency to make feasts into fiestas. The tendency is especially pronounced when feasts recur regularly in terms of the Catholic calendar and involve the entire común, but also can be noted in connection with such events as the shearing, the pig slaughter, and—according to older informants—spontaneous decisions on the part of several households to slaughter a lamb.

Commensal events involving the común appear to be of two kinds. Those which are today called pueblo fiestas are all celebrated on the same calendar day each year and are thus consistently identified as specific points in the Catholic calendar. The second kind of feast is also defined in terms of the Catholic year, but the dates differ from year to year. Into this latter category fall most of the feasts whose dates were established by auction bidding, designated by reference to the Catholic cycle but not necessarily recurring each year. I do not know if these were called pueblo fiestas in the past as the recurrent fiestas are today. They appear, however, to have assumed the dimensions of the pueblo fiestas which survive. Furthermore, in a given year, an ordinary fiesta might become a pueblo fiesta when, through auction bidding, it was designated as a date for meat sharing. This was the case on New Year's Day of 1884 (see pp. 44–45). San Antonio is now the only date on which some true (but partial) redistribution of meat takes place,[13] and it is associated with the recurrent annual business of pasture use. The "floating" fiestas designated during auctions have all disappeared, but San Antonio itself is exemplary of the association of mass, feast, and meeting which—though once more prevalent—still characterizes the setting of Valdemora's corporate activities.

A review of the full range of the común's activities, both modern ones and those known only through documents, indicates that its affairs are typically conducted in conjunction with the fiesta calendar. The village archive here serves to corroborate impressions based on the reduced number of pueblo fiestas still maintained. It appears that gatherings for business serve as excuses for feasting, and vice versa. Almost all records of council meetings are dated on known fiesta days, except for some of the series of auctions, most of which seem to have taken place near the turn of the year—from about mid-November to about mid-January. The bidding itself fixes dates for future feasts in terms of the Catholic calendar and thereby places them in a religious setting. All of the council's meetings on recurrent annual business are today held on various saints' days after mass: these include cendera (without a special mass), the annual meeting of the burial society after one of the two requiem masses said for it (at Corpus Christi and the second day of San Isidro), the annual accounting meeting of the Brotherhood of San Isidro on the second day of the fiesta or on the following Sunday, and the settling of pasture accounts on San Antonio. Other meetings, such as the one which establishes the irrigation schedule, are held either on Sundays or on the afternoon of some other fiesta day. San Roque and the days of the September fiesta, for example, have been occasions for

13. The redistribution of the San Antonio lamb is "partial" because the feast is attended only by active vecinos who today do not carry portions of the animal home, though evidence suggests that this was once done.

meetings on miscellaneous subjects. The accounting meetings at San Isidro and San Antonio have sometimes also covered miscellaneous business. Only true emergency business is handled on ordinary week days.

The village archive shows that there are several dates on which meetings were consistently held in the past, though it is more accurate to speak of clusters of dates, for any fiesta properly begins with the vespers of the previous evening, and, further, although events are scheduled with reference to certain fiesta days, there is some flexibility involved in the choice of a convenient day. The dates in the following list appear to have had council meetings associated with them in several different years.

| | |
|---|---|
| 7 October | Virgin María del Rosario |
| 10–12 November | San Martín |
| 21–22 November | |
| 1 December | |
| 8 December | Immaculate Conception |
| 15–17 December (especially 15) | |
| 31 December<br>1–2 January | New Year's Eve and Day |
| 28–30 January | |
| 20–23 February | |
| 15–17 March (especially 16) | |

As noted, some of these are still identified as fiesta dates. The significant recurrence of meetings on the other dates suggests that they, too, were once recognized fiestas, though no one can now testify to this fact. The designation of some of these days for the consumption of auction bids appears to have made of them full-scale pueblo fiestas. It also becomes apparent that the period of the most numerous pueblo fiestas neatly surrounds the period of the harvest, and the two major fiestas mark transitional points in the yearly ceremonial cycle, as well as in the economic cycle.

The mass-feast-meeting complex that gives pueblo fiestas their special character is crucial in binding together the separate households on the occasions when they must function jointly. The bonds of sentiment, mutual interest, cooperation, and obligation that hold together the nuclear family in its daily activities are not strong enough to bridge the gap between households, and it is precisely at times requiring collective participation that religious sanctions become operative. The imperatives of community action are thus religious imperatives as well. Participation is a duty as well as a privilege, and the proper fulfillment of one's duty to the community *makes* one a good Christian in Valdemoran terms. The man who continually failed in this duty would, in effect, fail to complete his share of the community's work and would thus lose the right to draw water at the fountain, to cut firewood, to use the village streets, to pasture his animals, or to share meat. The fact that such a man would also be failing as a Christian helps to insure that no one dare approach such an extreme—and in fact no one does.

The villagers' definition of a good Christian emphasizes harmonious participation in collective ritual and places little value on general compliance with Church dogma. Most villagers confess and take communion only once a year, at Easter, and attend mass only on fiesta days. On those days, the near-perfect attendance speaks for the stress on collective observance. The formal Church does not play a significant part in community life apart from its offering of services on those occasions which tradition vests with importance. Church-affiliated groups such as Catholic Action do not to my knowledge function in any of the Sierra villages. This is perhaps partly due to the villages' small size and the absence of a leisure class, but also to the fact that their citizenry is fully mobilized within the corporate village structure and has little need of what the Church offers. Village priests, too, are denied important roles in local affairs, and they are usually roundly disliked. Local custom supports the communities' distaste for even one annual confession to the resident priest by the importation of priests from other parishes to hear confessions at Easter. By choosing specifically to question the morality of pueblo fiestas, the priest I knew in Valdemora enjoyed unparalleled popularity as a scapegoat. His chief contribution to village life was in the creation of a schismogenic effect which strengthened the internal solidarity of the común and insured his exclusion from its affairs.

The institutions of formal Catholicism are hardly the focus of village religion, though emigrants appear to adapt easily to situations where religious life centers on the Church. In Valdemora, religious sanctions and ritual cluster closely around the activities which constrain the members of different families to act as one family in the execution of their common business. Feasting may be viewed as part of their business concerns, for it effects the redistribution of meat, but it is also a ceremonial expression of their common bonds. That the feast creates conviviality in an affair of necessity is part of its importance; and that the vecino cast aside the selfish concerns, the envy, and the grudges of his daily life is incumbent upon him as a member of an exclusive religious community. "Those who sit at meat together are united for all social effects; those who do not eat together are aliens to one another, without fellowship in religion and without reciprocal social duties."[14]

It is the villagers' view that the standards by which they conduct their daily lives are neither unrelated nor opposed to the imperatives which govern their fiesta conduct: daily conduct and fiesta conduct grow out of a single ideology. A rule of autonomy and even partial avoidance of one's neighbors helps to insure that frictions do not assume the proportions of social ruptures. The rule applies among vecinos as it does between brothers; within the común as within the family, people must live together. Fiestas at once grow out of the requirements of coexistence and invest them with positive value, temporarily making of the común a family.

The events involved in the celebration of San Antonio clearly illustrate the importance of the feast at a time of possible conflict of interests between vecinos. Although agricultural plots are all

14. W. Robertson Smith 1914, p. 269.

privately owned, customary law recognizes the right of access of the entire común to the produce of these plots in certain circumstances—that is, either when they lie fallow or after they have been harvested. The wild growth on fallow fields and the grain stubble on harvested fields constitute pasture resources to which all families' flocks are allowed access. (My use of the English *stubble* here includes both grain stubble and growth on fallow, unless otherwise noted, for both are treated alike for accounting purposes.)

The entry of stock into otherwise forbidden areas is known in Spain as the *derrota*. Where it is practiced it is intimately associated with coordinated field rotation within communities; stubble-grazing in these situations is distinct from that where individual herders contract with individual farmers for entry into certain fields.[15] The derrota involves a community of individuals as herders vis à vis the same community of individuals as farmers. If all families cultivated equal amounts and had flocks of equal size, stubble-grazing would raise no problems. But given inequalities in both areas, some vecinos are giving more in pasturage than they are receiving in fodder for their own animals, and some flocks are consuming more than their owners are making available to others. (The deposition of fertilizer and its benefit to the farmer are considered functions of flock size and field size, respectively, and do not receive separate attention.) The proceedings at San Antonio are designed to correct this imbalance.[16]

Until 1961, the balancing of accounts was as much symbolic as financial. Each vecino's debt to the House of Medinaceli for pasture was assessed in proportion to the number of animals he grazed that season. Larger stock owners thus paid more of the

15. See, for example, Campbell 1964.

16. The adjustment of pasturage accounts within the community accompanies the collection of ducal rents in all of the surrounding villages on the day of San Antonio. It seems likely that the derrota once involved all of the villages of the cuadrilla and that the livestock count for entry into the stubble for all their flocks was coordinated on San Antonio.

rent (which does not cover growth on private plots). The cost of a feast (a choice lamb, vegetables, drink, fruit, and tobacco) was divided by the same proportions, so that the larger stock owners were automatically paying for most of the feast of which all vecinos partook equally. This was deemed sufficient compensation for stubble. The system was better adapted to an earlier period when every family kept at least a small flock, and a note of recent change must be added here. The lessening of dependency on flocks for meat has recently caused serious imbalances in flock sizes. Although the total number of sheep in town has been fairly stable (approximately nine hundred to one thousand head) for at least two centuries, in 1963 the majority of animals belonged to four owners with flocks exceeding two hundred head each, two vecinos had exceedingly small flocks, and the rest had no sheep at all. Thus, there was rising discontent with the inadequacy of the feast in covering the real debt owed the nonherders by the large herders. In 1962, the vecinos made counts not only of livestock, but also of the number of hectares each vecino had in fallow and stubble that year. The provinces annually set a cash value on the hectare of stubble. The total value of stubble and ducal pasture rental is divided by the number of animals and a price per animal derived.[17] Thus, the price of both ducal pasture and stubble is divided proportionally among stock owners, and nonherders actually receive cash for the difference owed them. This new system makes the feast obsolete, just as the feasts scheduled by auctions have been made obsolete by commercial butchering. In this instance, however, the vecinos decided to maintain the feast "so as not to lose the custom," though none of them is certain how long the tradition can persist.

San Antonio is the most important surviving example of the true redistributive feasts with associated council meetings. As certain kinds of business have vanished from the council's agenda,

17. Actually, grazing units rather than animals are counted: sheep are one unit each and draft animals and goats five units each. The figures are based on both amounts and types of pasture consumed.

so have the associated celebrations disappeared. But some fiestas have the less tangible, but no less important feature of integrating members into the común structure and reinforcing the tight boundaries by which the común is defined. The ceremonial events which are associated with the maintenance of the común itself have not disappeared from the calendar and deserve attention here.

Although parts of a person's progress in the Church and of his life cycle are paid little heed in village tradition, some of these events are regarded as being of general import and are accompanied by special observances in the común. Thus there exist, as I have mentioned, communal aspects of the family fiestas accompanying baptism, first communion, and marriage, and also of funerals. It is possible to view these traditions as giving symbolic recognition to the individual's passage from one to another corporate status within the structure of the común, to the crossing of común boundaries, and to the passage at death out of the structure.

In chapter 2, I have said that the passage into the group of mozos at age seventeen and the entrance into the común at marriage or at the attainment of adult bachelor's status are marked by the payment of entrance fees, which are usually assessed in terms of foodstuffs to be consumed jointly by the members of the group involved. The baptism of a child of a común family is the infant's public debut as well as its entry into the Church. Although the baptismal ceremony and the party following it are open only to kin and friends by invitation and do not involve the whole común, one of the associated traditions appears to be of a different order. The children of the village (boys and girls under seventeen) come as a group to the house of the infant's family while the baptismal party is gathered there after the ceremony. Much in the trick-or-treat style which characterizes the children's Christmas caroling and the mozos' begging for supper on the night of cendera, the children raise a clamor at the door and demand sweets or coins, or both, from inside. Either the infant's father or the godfather is responsible for throwing handfulls of these into the crowd of children, who scramble for them before leaving the family fiesta in peace. Villagers respond positively to the suggestion of a symbolic parallel between the events at baptism and the later payment of entrance fees to one's peers. The later payments for entrance are by definition commensal affairs, for mozos or vecinos, when new members are incorporated.

The date on which the celebration of first communion is fixed for any village children ready for the event is usually an ordinary fiesta in the spring, such as Corpus Christi. This by definition brings the entire común to mass. Although in all other respects the event is celebrated only in the kin group, the very fact that the event is coordinated for different families and scheduled on a fiesta gives it some place in the cycle of village-wide celebrations.

The announcement of wedding banns signals the final step in formal engagement and the impending separation of mozo and moza from their respective groups. After the mass occasioning the first announcement of banns, the prospective bride and groom each receives his age-mates in his home and offers liqueurs and sweets. When bride and groom are from different villages, banns are announced on the same three consecutive Sunday (or fiesta) masses in both village churches, and the receptions for mozos and mozas take place in the villages of groom and bride, respectively.

The wedding itself is a family fiesta in Valdemora. Weddings traditionally take place in the bride's village, but today almost all Sierra villagers are married in Sigüenza. I refer here to the traditional village wedding, for the removal of the entire proceedings to Sigüenza (in about the last ten years) has made continued communal participation in the event impossible. (Here I distinguish continued practices by use of the present tense.) The wedding ceremony—the civil ceremony at the church door and the religious one before the altar—is attended only by invited guests: certain friends of the bride and groom and kinsmen of each. The number of invitations made depends upon the parents' ability and desire to pay for a large wedding. The principles according to which guests are invited have not changed; they are the principles appropriate to a family and not a común affair. The number of kinsmen invited is not determined by recognized differences in degrees of genealogical relationship, but by considerations of sentiment and expense.

All of the substantive sharing of food is limited to the group of guests. The pueblo wedding ceremony was traditionally followed by a breakfast in the bride's house. Afterward, certain kinds of foods were shared in public (in the plaza, or in an enclosed public place in bad weather) with the común as a whole: toasted hempseeds, cakes, and a sweetened wine sopeta like that shared at San Roque. Hired musicians perform for the public part of the wedding, which became a village-wide dance. The dance was disbanded for the main meal in the afternoon, when invited guests returned to the bride's home to eat. The dance resumed in the late afternoon and lasted much of the night, when it was the express purpose of the mozos and mozas in particular to prevent the newlyweds from going to bed. The festivities continued when the newlyweds retired. Traditional wedding festivities lasted until the afternoon of the day following the ceremony. On the second day, as on the first, festive breakfast and noonday meals were served the guests, with a dance intervening. After the afternoon meal, invited guests from elsewhere returned to their own villages.

The proceedings of the wedding night were complicated in cases of intervillage marriages, for then representatives of two competing mozo groups were present and the usual competitive atmosphere of such encounters was heightened by the fact that a mozo of the visiting group had just married a native moza and been assessed a fine for so doing. The threatened intrusion had become real, and the confrontation of the two mozo groups at a wedding involved a recognition of foreign invasion of village boundaries.[18] An endogamous match, on the other hand, involved only the recognition of a loss in membership for mozos and mozas

18. The crossing of village boundaries here parallels the crossing of kingroup boundaries necessitated by any Sarakatsan marriage (Campbell 1964), and the nature of the resulting antagonism, particularly between the young men, is similar. However, Campbell reports the outbreak of actual hostilities at Sarakatsan weddings, whereas in the Sierra Ministra, "hostilities" are carefully kept in the realm of verbal banter and more or less good-humored pranks.

and attention centered largely on the joking attempt to prevent the sexual consummation which accompanies the couple's change in status. The change is shortly thereafter celebrated among the vecinos at the feast by which the newly married man becomes incorporated into the group of household heads.

Illness and death concern the común as well as the family. The común acts corporately in its capacity as burial society in the respects already mentioned: the adra is activated during grave illness or at death; attendance at funerals is required of all members; the burial society generally pays for funeral masses; graves are dug by adra; and members of the común all join with outsiders to offer condolences at the house of the bereaved family immediately following the burial. But the burial society's activity with respect to a deceased member ends on the day of the funeral. The bereaved family alone is responsible for scheduling and paying for the commemorative masses offered on succeeding days and, later, for the yearly commemorative masses. These masses are not attended by the común; close kin of the deceased may, on the other hand, travel from other villages to attend them. Novenas following the death are similarly attended—by women of the común as friends, by few común men, and by outsiders. As mentioned, none of these events is regarded as commensal by nature (though the bereaved family feeds its visitors from other villages) and no special foods are associated with death or funerals. The obligation to wear mourning for a prolonged period rests with specific kinsmen of the deceased—with his siblings and with his lineal ascendants and descendants, with his spouse and his spouse's siblings and lineal ascendants and descendants, but with no collateral kin in either case, even if they are also members of the común. The period of mourning varies with age, sex, and relationship to the deceased, and in general the severity of the rules is today being relaxed. (Mourners also kneel when nonmourners do not at one point in the mass.)

The burial society is activated twice yearly on occasions other than funerals. It orders two requiem masses said in its name, in commemoration of deceased members, and attendance is again required. On one of these occasions the society holds its annual business meeting, recording fines and filling out its accounts. The masses are presently associated with Corpus Christi and the second day of the San Isidro fiesta.

A century ago, the two requiem masses were said on the Octava del Señor (1 January, the Feast of the Circumcision) and on the feast of the Virgin María del Rosario. More recent history has witnessed a good deal of manipulation of the fiesta schedule, indicating the ease with which Valdemorans shift events from one date to another, always with reference to fiestas recognized in that period. Today, María del Rosario is no longer celebrated and 1 January has no special observances associated with it, though we know both were more important in the past. Vecinos do not remember the association of burial society masses with these dates. I was told in 1963 that until about five years earlier there had been no fixed dates for the second requiem mass, and the burial society meeting took place after the requiem mass on Corpus Christi. At that time also, the fiesta of San Isidro was a one-day affair, and the September fiesta lasted three days. The vecinos decided to take one day from the September fiesta and add it to San Isidro; at that time they fixed the second requiem mass and the burial society meeting for the second day of San Isidro. In the year I was told this, however, the requiem mass took place on the fixed day, but the business meeting was instead held on the first day of the September fiesta!

The lesson to the field worker is, first, that documents state as fixed facts things which their authors themselves regard as less fixed. More important, there is little evidence for general constancy in much of the fiesta calendar. Although there is evidence for the celebration of San Isidro for over a century, there is none for the September fiesta, for it is not associated with corporate functions about which records have been left. Among the pueblo fiestas, San Roque, and those observed by subgroups of the común (such as Todos los Santos and the Holy Week complex) appear quite old, but we have seen the schedule of many fiestas associated with meat redistribution to be more flexible. In any case, it appears traditional that the burial society recognize two annual ceremonial events involving its membership, regardless of the specific fiestas on which these occur.

The requiem masses may be seen as honoring the burial society as a whole in its corporate continuity, the living buying masses for all the dead members, and separating members from nonmembers by their participation on these occasions. The focus of these occasions is of a different order from the society's ad hoc functions in rendering aid to single member families. Similarly, the special gatherings of subgroups of the común, usually with the sharing of food within them, such as the mozos' supper after cendera or on the eve of Easter and the mozos' and mozas' involvement in both San Juan and Todos los Santos; and the obligations of niños on Easter, and mozas and mozos on San Isidro (described presently), can all be viewed in much the same light as the burial society's two yearly functions. They cement the membership through common activities (and food sharing) and bring their corporate status into clear focus by the forceful exclusion of the nonmembers who are, in daily life, their playmates and companions outside the común or their elders or juniors within it.

These last points bring us to a consideration of the fiesta of the patron saint, San Isidro. Again, the proceedings have little to do with the saint himself, and elements of the complex associated with this fiesta have parallels on different dates in neighboring villages. The Hermandad de San Isidro is the only corporate association in Valdemora which has no explicit mutual-aid or overt regulatory functions. Membership in it is automatic with entrance into the común; the newly entered vecino is initiated immediately into the office of mayordomo, which otherwise rotates on the basis of común seniority and never by adra; and the organization is activated solely for the annual celebration of San Isidro.

The mayordomo's family is responsible for making the large,

ring-shaped cakes *(rollos)* which are important in the fiesta, and the mayordomo handles the fiesta finances. The following description is based on the 1963 proceedings. Común households (including widows and retired vecinos) each contribute two *celemines* of wheat flour or its cash equivalent. (The celemín is the twelfth part of a fanega, or about three and two-thirds kilograms.) In 1963, four outsiders who deal regularly with the pueblo also contributed "the pair," as it is called: the priest, the station restaurateur, the storekeeper, and the Medinaceli doctor—the only four individuals who have limited roles as quasi-patrons to villagers.[19] The mayordomo's fiesta treasury pays for additional ingredients for the cakes, for wine and anise, for candles for the saint, for fireworks, for plaza decorations, for the cost of the church services, and for items to adorn the oak bough featured at the fiesta. The mozos alone pay the hired musicians' fee.

On the day before the fiesta, the cakes are baked; these numbered fifty-four in 1963, aside from three unusually large ones, specially decorated—two to hang on the bough and one to be placed at the feet of the saint. The mozos go into the hills on this afternoon to select a handsome bough. They are given a fresh cake to eat on their journey. Also, on the eve of the fiesta, the mayordomo invites his successor for the following year, the priest, and the alcalde and his assistant officers to his home, where they divide one of the cakes and drink wine together. On the morning of 15 May, before the mass, the mozos gather in the plaza to decorate the bough with cakes and with oranges and lemons. This activity is accompanied by the consumption of another cake and a bottle of anise. The decorated bough is placed in the church and blessed by the priest. The contributors of flour each receive two of the cakes, two are saved to be eaten at the mayordomo's accounting meeting, and the remainder are saved

19. The four have no contractual patron-client relations with Valdemorans and might better be called "brokers" than "patrons" in the strict sense.

to be auctioned in the afternoon, with one cake for the officials' table at the auction.

The solemn mass, with the assistance of two visiting priests, features a procession with the saint. The procession pauses at a spot overlooking the garden plots, where the priest blesses the village fields, before returning the saint to the church.

The afternoon auction is the last event considered traditional (except the requiem mass of the next day), and the evening and the entire second day after mass are devoted to public dances, visiting within families, organized games for children, and a general men's shooting match. The items auctioned are the plain and decorated cakes, the oranges and lemons from the bough, and sometimes the bough itself. The proceeds of the auction are returned to the Hermandad's treasury, kept by the various mayordomos in turn. The auctioneer's table seats the four officers of the ayuntamiento, the priest, the civil guard on duty for the fiesta, and miscellaneous others involved in organizing fiesta events. This group enjoys cake and wine during the event and is responsible for recording the proceedings and collecting the bids.

The events culminating in the auction were changed after 1963, but this primarily involved a reshuffling of the traditional features. Instead of contributing flour, the usual donors now contribute one cake apiece as "a gift to the saint." The mayordomo's wife makes only the decorated cakes. (This relieves the one family of an excessive burden, and the other households order their cakes from a lot made by the baker.) The oak bough is more heavily decorated than before; it bears the cakes contributed by the común households, oranges and lemons, and such luxury goods as packaged candies and tins of the locally famous Soria butter or Guadalajara honey. In the days preceding the fiesta, the mozas are charged with selling tickets for a lottery, which replaces the auction procedure for disposing of the laden oak bough. The drawing takes place in front of the church after the mass and procession. At one peseta per ticket, and with the Spanish love of lotteries, the fiesta treasury has benefited from the change, though the auction, too, brought in much more than the actual worth of the items involved.

At the auction, where participation was more easily documented than in the purchase of lottery tickets, the chief bidders were almost invariably outsiders to the común. The fiesta is interesting in that it places some common features of común proceedings in a ceremonial context where their substance changes. Thus, the auction, which is normally redistributive by nature, is explicitly not redistributive here: it deals primarily with specialty foods which are exchanged with outsiders, who appear to adopt a means of thanking their host village by making these purchases at outrageous prices. (The lottery permits much cheaper participation.) The común officials and the mozos accompany all their fiesta activities with food and drink, as is usual, but these are hardly the substantial foodstuffs associated with most of the rest of the fiesta cycle; they are again specialty foods—rollos and drink. And the vecinos do not feast together as a group; on this occasion alone, the group is represented at table by its officialdom only.

In strong contrast to the redistributive feasts like San Antonio, all of the events which I have viewed here as marking individual changes in corporate status or emphasizing the boundaries of corporate membership take place in conjunction with family fiestas (or funerals) or family gatherings on ordinary fiestas when the pueblo is filled with outsiders. Thus, at baptisms, weddings, and funerals, on the occasions when requiem masses are held, and at San Isidro, the común stakes its claim on its members in contexts where the kin group is present to make competing claims. Similarly, the activities of the smaller subgroups, such as mozos, derive much of their style and intensity from the presence of competing groups, from either within the común or outside it. The tradition of trick-or-treating, or the raucous demand for food, which accompanies some of these activities can be seen as a demand by a junior group for corporate recognition by a senior one, for food is the medium through which corporate status is both achieved and maintained. It is only the adult men, however, who, as household heads, control the food supply and have the power to effect its redistribution. Younger groups must beg from their parents.[20]

The events of corporate life which juxtapose members against outsiders, whether with reference to the whole común or to parts of it, involve the use of food on a less substantial but a highly symbolic level. These events sometimes involve the passage of foodstuffs across the lines to outsiders—between villages, as at the former Charity of San Roque or when a mozo pays a fee to the mozos of another común, or between juniors and seniors (or the two sexes) within the común. Indeed, this is a point which makes apparent the possibility of classifying fiestas on the basis of the type of foodstuffs involved. The sharing of meat is restricted to the gatherings of the kin-group alone in the confines of a house or to the gatherings of the común alone without outsiders—and these events may be classified as real meals. Food sharing which involves neither meat nor full-scale meals occurs in contexts where the celebrants are not alone and where some attention is necessarily focused on the boundaries between their own and other groups. Foods shared in these contexts belong predominantly to the bread, wine, and sweets complex which is ritually and symbolically important throughout most of the Mediterranean and much of the rest of Europe.

A classification of fiestas by the foods involved, which is sometimes implicit in native usage, yields the breakdown of the list of fiestas shown in table 3. Its major interest lies in the division into two types of the category which Valdemorans call pueblo fiestas. The ones occasioning common meals are those which activate the redistributive powers of the adult males of the común. The entrance into vecino status is the only event marking passage

20. The tradition of egg-stealing by the group of bachelors in the Hungarian village of Átány (Fél and Hofer 1969) can be seen in the same light. Átány shows important parallels with Valdemora in many aspects of its corporate structure and in the traditions surrounding joint action of the village and its corporate subgroups.

TABLE 3

Ceremonial Events Classified with Respect to Commensal Traditions

| In Kin Groups | In Común and/or Subgroups |
|---|---|
| **Common Meals** | |
| First communion | San Antonio and other feasts determined by auctions[a] (vecinos) |
| Wedding | Entrance to vecino status (vecinos) |
| Ordinary fiestas: | |
| San Isidro | |
| September fiesta | |
| National fiestas | |
| Sundays[b] | |
| Shearing | |
| Pig slaughter | |
| **Bread-Wine-Sweets** | |
| Baptism | Baptism (niños, niñas) |
| Wedding | Wedding (común and subgroups) |
| | Wedding banns (mozos, mozas) |
| | Entrance to mozo status (mozos) |
| | Foreign mozo fee payment (mozos) |
| | Mozas' birthdays (mozas) |
| | San Juan (mozos, mozas) |
| | Todos los Santos (mozos, mozas) |
| | Jueves Lardero (mozos, mozas) |
| | Cendera supper (vecinos, mozos) |
| | Easter eve (mozos) |
| | San Isidro (común and subgroups) |
| | San Roque (común and subgroups) |
| **No Food** | |
| Funeral | Funeral (común) |
| | Burial society masses (vecinos and wives) |

[a] Cf. pp. 44 and 96.

[b] Sundays are not always commensal in the sense of all other events listed here—i.e., including members of separate households at table—but they often become so by virtue of their status as days of rest.

through the común structure, or the crossing of boundaries, which involves a full-scale meal. This is significant because it is, of course, the event which marks a man's attainment of redistributive powers through membership in the town council. On other occasions of meriendas or suppers among members of the común, the featured foods are either bread, wine, or sweets, or—as in the suppers after cendera—the foods are supplied in small portions by all households. The sandwiches for such meriendas never contain the mutton on which redistributive processes center, but rather eggs, pork products, or cheese.

The importance of both San Isidro and San Roque in its old form can be seen in their activation of the entire común as well as various of its subgroups. San Roque is a pueblo fiesta, in contrast to San Isidro, for the sopeta is consumed by members of the común together in a public place. But the evidence from the past shows that—much like San Isidro—it once activated the común more extensively than it does today. Four mayordomos served each year, by adra, to finance and organize the charity of bread and cheese. The fiesta was an explicit expression of goodwill toward outsiders; neighboring villagers remember it as a major event, and the fiesta is still regarded as an occasion of special hilarity within the común. The charity was discontinued largely because the size of the resident railroad community guaranteed such a large number of outsiders that the cost became prohibitive. Like the auction of San Isidro, the charity confronted the común directly with a group of outsiders. In contrast to the San Isidro auction, the passage of foodstuffs from the común to its visitors was totally nonreciprocal, even on a token level. The outsiders were cast into a subordinate role reminiscent of that of the itinerant beggar. The men of the común doled out fixed portions of bread and cheese to all comers, who filed in line before their hosts' table and thanked them formally before leaving the común alone to share its sopeta and hold its dance together.[21] The patronizing style of the charity would be offensive to the kinsmen of común members, but the San Roque charity is for miscellaneous outsiders

21. Today the women still distribute sopeta to children and miscellaneous outsiders: the style is similar to, but less formal than, that of the men's cheese giving.

and the members of "competing" neighbor villages, and it calls to mind the verse in which Valdemorans deride the standard of living of their immediate neighbors:

| | |
|---|---|
| El hambre nació en Salcedo, | Hunger was born in Salcedo, |
| Por Aguasalida se pasó, | Through Aguasalida it passed, |
| Hizo noche en Algarabejo, | Spent the night in Algarabejo, |
| Y en Medina se quedó. | And in Medina came to rest. |

To envoys from "hostile" foreign villages, the charity could express both pity and Valdemora's own superiority.

This excursion through the fiesta calendar shows how the events of village life requiring cooperation between households are part of a mass-feast-meeting complex which places them in a religious setting and brings to bear on the participants the sanctions associated with their duties as Christians. There are few events of a ceremonial nature which do not in some way concern the whole común, though they may also concern individual kin groups, and the entire inventory of ceremonial events is weighted heavily toward collective rather than individual observances. Those things for which households depend on one another—the redistribution of meat and the administration of other collective affairs—are so closely associated with the events of the fiesta cycle as to be inseparable from it. And so, too, individuals are ceremonially welded into associations which cross household lines and create a village-wide arena of interaction. The fact that corporate action is one with religious observance guarantees the degree of internal control which allows the común to function independently of the formal political and judicial framework of which it is nominally a part.

Analysis of the fiesta cycle clearly indicates the units of the social organization which have the most important roles in the maintenance of order. The común is the largest unit which is able to muster the unmitigated loyalty of all its component parts and whose members are in their own view coreligious. The común is, in the small villages of this region, the corporate body of a single municipality—a tract of territory under a single administration; and in these villages the limits of the municipality *are the limits of the religious parish,* with no internal subdivisions. The "dependent" hamlet is no less independent an entity than the seat of the ayuntamiento; the despoblado governs itself as does its larger neighbor. Each of these units is a separate municipality governed by a separate común de vecinos, each with its own church and unique calendar of fiestas. Both as a separate parish and as the only indivisible territorial unit,[22] the municipality has a religious identity which at once unites its inhabitants and creates a gulf between them and their neighbors. The symbolic content of such fiestas as San Isidro and San Roque, and the encounters of mozos across village lines whenever they occur, show beyond doubt that the relations of común to común, in contrast to corporate relations within a común, are of a new and inherently competitive order. On no observable or documentable occasion does a larger unit subsume común loyalties, and units like the defunct pasturage league lived and died at the will of their constituent corporations. The fact that such organizations were simply federations of the truly crucial structural units is evidenced not only by their total lapse from local memory and locally recorded history, but also by the comparable structure of existing federations for other purposes (cf. chapter 2).

The unity of the común is expressed on yet another level, in people's references to the común as a family, or a group of relatives, and in their notion that the ideals of familial harmony should bear upon común life. Valdemorans' notion of their kinship within the común must be regarded as something of a social fiction, for

22. The farm villages of the Sierra Ministra appear too small to support formal internal subdivisions, either of distinct neighborhoods (barrios), which usually have some separate religious identity; or in the formal religious structure (separate parishes); or in the associational structure where multiple organizations like burial societies or other confraternities would have to compete with one another for members. This problem is reviewed elsewhere (Freeman 1968a and b).

the links between all families cannot be traced by a single informant. Instead, people say that in such a small town where families have long histories, all families *must* be related to one another. Genealogical ties are assumed, but the notion of kinship is independent of the proof of such ties. There are two major blocs of families (see endsheets) which no informant can link together. This separates modern Households 8, 15, 16, and 17 from the others. The two blocs are actually related through a sibling tie in the eldest generation on the chart. The particular tie has been forgotten, though other contemporaries of that period appear in many genealogies.

Neither of the two notions of broad kinship which I shall discuss depends upon knowledge of the genealogical facts which, ironically, can usually be traced quite easily. One notion of blood kinship binds the members of the común, regardless of their other ties. The second notion links families in networks across village lines and excludes some común families from each other's networks. Kinship networks will be treated in the next chapter. But I must emphasize now that *both* notions of kinship involve some social fictions in the more distant degrees, though a factual basis for assumed ties is often discoverable. Rather than tracing actual links, family X identifies itself with families Y and Z, through either blood or sometimes only affinal links, and sometimes by common surnames as well. By extension, then, members of family X are "somewhat related" *(algo de familia)* to any blocs of families with which Y or Z recognize links. There are no boundaries in the definition of kinship; different individuals and families may have more or less extensive knowledge of ties and more or less interest in claiming extensive ties. There are no recognized obligations between categories of kin other than those who mourn for one another (see p. 104), and many of these are not binding. The activation of relationships on the basis of kinship is largely a question of choice and always dependent upon the social context. The Ocens of Valdemora may recognize no relationship with the bloc of Ocen-related families in Mazarulleque, partly because their feelings about that town lead them to deny ties with it, whereas they do recognize kinship with the Gutierrez bloc in Aguasalida, but again none with the Guiterrez bloc in Valdemora. In those contexts where común membership is conceived as one of kinship, however, the Ocen and Gutierrez families of Valdemora claim at least that they are "somewhat related." In these contexts people are members of a "family"; in other contexts they are "relatives" or "related."

Family reputations, based on local memory, may ordinarily influence one family's wish or refusal to claim ties with another; but when the común acts as a family, there is no choice. There is choice only when a family's known roots are far enough away that there is no basis for assuming blood relationship. The family in Household 1 (endsheets) falls into this category, as its head came to the común as a vecino's stepson. The fact that his deceased father apparently had a bad reputation reinforces the gap between him and other común members; in addition, his stepfather's father before him had entered the común only at marriage and not by birth. This vecino apparently both expects treatment as a marginal member and does little to discourage it. His status in the común cannot be glossed over by any fiction. Although he is one of the most boisterous leaders at fiesta proceedings, he is also the single most vociferous source of discord in some of the council's business proceedings. His case points to Valdemorans' implicit demand that there must be some plausible basis for assuming ties between families, and (in the absence of known ties) a documented history far from Valdemora makes the claim of kinship unsupportable. It is this feature which also separates virtually the entire railroad community from the pueblo.

Común Households 8, 15, 16, and 17 (endsheets) all descend from outsiders who bought land in the común, and yet these people are not considered foreigners in any sense. Partly, their forerunners' known origins in nearby towns might allow the assumption of blood ties in any case; partly, the length of their history in town permits them to claim, with the other households, that they "descend from Valdemora." Time, no doubt, would permit the descendants of Household 1 the same claim.

Pitt-Rivers's comments on the quality of relations between kinsmen in an Andalusian town are of interest here for the one element of contrast which Valdemora presents in an otherwise similar situation:

> the lack of mutual rights and obligations outside the elementary family, the lack even of occasions on which the unity of the extended family is expressed . . . makes of kinship a facultative rather than a firm bond. It is an excellent basis for friendship, but is not in itself an important element in the structure of this society.[23]

The crucial difference in Valdemora is that there is a single kind of context in which kinship is a binding and not a merely facultative tie: these are the contexts in which membership in the territorial unit, the común, becomes the focus of economic and religious activity, raising the otherwise moot issue of genealogical ties beyond the realm of doubt and creating an arena of behavior in which común members are bound as kinsmen. In larger and more stratified communities than are to be found in the Sierra Ministra, such contexts are lacking, for these communities are usually not mobilized *in their entirety* (that is involving every household directly) in a single corporate structure.[24]

The fact that notions of común kinship, of economic interdependence, and of cooperative harmony in Valdemora are specific to the realm of corporate life points to the true importance of the territorial unit in defining a sphere of action to which certain definitions of relationships and behavioral constraints are appropriate. An analysis of villagers' social relationships must of necessity be a contextual one. Valdemorans themselves recognize the dual quality in their social life. A vecino on his way to the harvest on the morning after the sopeta said to me wistfully, "Today isn't San Roque." It is hardly surprising that corporate social life, be-

23. Pitt-Rivers 1961:106.
24. Freeman 1968a.

cause it is not the totality of social life and imposes ideals which are not active in other contexts, depends ultimately upon religious sanctions to make binding the claims of kinship and interdependence of the común members. Yet it would be wrong to view the idea of común kinship solely as a myth invoked on occasion by a group of neighbors, for there is a real assumption of real ties, to which the present exclusion of Household 1 attests.

The común is neatly circumscribed by two terminological usages. First, the terms for uncle *(tío)* and aunt *(tía)* are applied to the oldest members by all their juniors, for both reference and address, except by their lineal descendants and their spouses, who call them as parents or grandparents. The extension of the *kinship* terms *tío* and *tía* to común elders does not mean that they are regarded as "uncles" and "aunts." In addition to their use for parents' and grandparents' siblings and their spouses, these terms also refer specifically to "non-blood kin" who have been grafted onto families. For example, a man will call his father "*padre*," but his father's second wife, his own stepmother, he calls "tía." This young man's wife calls her husband's father "*abuelo*" ("grandfather"), but her husband's stepmother "tía." All común seniors are called by this special term, whereas people of comparable age in the station barrio or in other villages are not referred to in this way. The usage stops at the boundaries of the común itself.

The second usage, the use of nicknames, circumscribes the común also, but in this case by its application only to outsiders, and occupational nicknames predominate. The fact that común members do not have nicknames is interesting, especially since Pitt-Rivers and Kenny have both documented their extensive use in two more heterogeneous communities and have suggested that they play a role in social control and the expression of community censure.[25] In Valdemora, the unit to which the tightest social controls pertain, the común, appears to dispense with nicknames and, instead, to use them to accentuate the boundaries between insiders and outsiders, between those who farm the municipality

25. Pitt-Rivers 1961; Kenny 1962.

and those who are there pursuing other occupations. In view of the contrast with the practices described for other towns, I submitted the question of nicknames to several members of the común. Their own opinion was that the town was too small to produce the duplication of Christian names that would make nicknames useful. (Nicknames are indeed more common in larger neighboring towns.) They also pointed out that their own use of nicknames was often in cases where they did not know people's real names (that is, in the itinerant elements of the railroad and commercial community). They were, however, able to quote nicknames based on personal or family (not occupational) characteristics in neighboring towns and, in one case only, for a deceased vecino of Valdemora who had an unusually colorful history (and who, perhaps significantly, left no descendants in the village who might defend his memory). It is plausible to suppose that Valdemora is indeed too small to support the use of nicknames—not only for the reason given by the villagers, but also because it is in the very nature of such appellations publicly to set individuals and families off from their fellows, while it is in the very nature of the común's public face to stress its members' common bonds.

As might be expected, the most serious disagreements in local memory have occurred between parties who are not bound in the común, or in contexts where individuals are not so bound—that is, in private family affairs. In recent memory there has been one quarrel over inheritance, which never reached formal proportions. In this case, a house was left as a mejora to a feeble-minded heir, and his sister tried unsuccessfully to contest the fact. The family reputation is tainted by this memory; but, oddly, the family involved were siblings of the stepfather of the infamous Household 1, and the stepson, who has a bad reputation anyway, is the only person left in town to carry the family burden. It is tempting to ask if villagers are not rather selective in cherishing bad memories with which to diminish his status—that is, whether "bad reputation" is not sometimes an ex post facto explanation of bad behavior. The vecino in question taxes the común's tolerance to its limits, and considerable ambivalence surrounds discussion of him to outsiders, for he *is* a member. I lived several months in Valdemora before people began to talk freely about him.

Another family quarrel is currently brewing. A man with children by two marriages is arguing with his second wife about the proper division of the estate, because the house itself, as well as the estate's productivity, have been much improved since a preliminary division of all property was recorded when the son became a vecino. Since the children of the second marriage are both daughters, married and living elsewhere, the son is heir to the house itself, and his stepmother's claim is that the daughters deserve more compensation than they are destined to receive. Were this a question only of the cash value of house and fields, the issue would perhaps be less serious. But the quarrel revolves around the less tangible issue of assessing the daughters' contribution to the estate's improvement over the thirty-odd years of the second marriage, for the daughters "worked for the house" and worked hard until their marriage. Assessment of the "facts" is not easy. It is felt that if the wife dies first, the husband will take his son's part. If the husband dies first, the widow is expected to mobilize her power over the estate in favor of her daughters. The implicit threat here, and the fear of all observers, is that there might be in either case a scandalous recourse to those freedoms permitted under the civil code and thus a breach of customary law. The heirs themselves could compromise to prevent such a turn of events; to date the quarrel is between the parents. The pueblo looks upon the whole matter with great apprehension: such things, it is said, happen only in Mazarulleque.[26] Things are made more difficult because each side has a good case, which all observers admit. The whole pueblo is aware of the problem, for it arises out

26. Mazarulleque is a scapegoat village in the immediate region. It is among the larger Sierra villages, and in many of these, disputes are more frequent than in their smaller neighbors (though I cannot cite actual numbers of court cases there). It is still important to remember Caro Baroja's directive (1957) that, in view of strong sociocentrism, it is the fieldworker's responsibility not to take at face value what any Spanish village says about its neighbors.

of the very essence of second marriages, and everyone is reticent to discuss it, for it threatens to touch the whole village with its ugliness. One of the important features of común power over its members is that the son, who must continue to live *in loco,* may be easily disposed to compromise with his half-sisters, for his public face depends upon it.

In relations with resident outsiders, and especially with the railroad community, común members tend to explain away unpleasant incidents by reference to the barbarity of foreigners. An alcalde once had to call the Civil Guard when two railroad workers fought in the bar and began to bite each other; they were taken to court in Aguasalida. People cite this only case of legal recourse with a knowing smile, for it is about "them" and represents such un-vecino-like behavior that it cannot possibly involve the face of the común.

The común as a body tries to gloss over differences with the station barrio when they occur. The situation is always ripe for an outbreak of resentment, and the vecinos recognize this and staunchly refuse to press issues which they feel are minor. For example, several non-pueblo women regularly wash at the lavadero, but do not take part in the women's adra to clean it (though non-común women who live in the pueblo do participate). Although the water supply is public by law, the fountain and lavadero are común-owned structures and the común considers all who use them liable for their maintenance and repair. Similarly, any resident outsider or child of the pueblo who owns or rents a garden plot is integrated into the irrigation adra in some arbitrary order, and they must observe their turns. Where even vecinos may argue about violations, relations with outsiders are even more potentially explosive. Again, the común has resolutely turned its back on the fact that some outsiders who live near the gardens draw their household water from the stream reserved for irrigation. While this act is not illegal, it is not proper in común terms, and outsiders tempt judgment in this way. No común family uses stream water for purposes other than irrigation. For the fiesta of San Isidro, the station barrio decided in 1963 to sponsor special events and entertainment for children, and also the shooting match. When their committee assessed pueblo as well as station households for a share in the costs, the farmers grumbled that común children were in very low proportion for the amount they were being asked to pay; but they paid. And, finally, the común has balked at some outside demands that cendera cover jobs which the vecinos do not consider their sole responsibility. For example, the vecinos point out that the high quality of road maintenance necessary for good access to the station cannot fall solely upon the común but must fall partly to the railroad and to the Ministry of Public Works. No one contests this assertion, but there is some question about who has jurisdiction over some of the roads, for some throughways recently defined as public access roads actually traverse one side of the pueblo and pass the fountain. At one point, a piece of government road machinery remained stationary for many weeks pending a question of jurisdiction. When active road work or dormant machinery impinge physically upon the pueblo, irritation can run high regardless of who finances the work. The común is called upon to do cendera in the church-school complex also, although this is government and not village property. In these instances, no one begrudges the church or school the hours of labor, but the común receives no help at all from the outsiders who in fact make greater proportional use of the facilities.

In all of these respects, as in other ways also, the presence of outsiders has created issues which do not exist in most other villages. The saving factor is perhaps the physical separation of the two communities. Women may see one another more often, but most contact between the two populations—and especially their men—occurs at Sunday mass, on Sunday afternoons when men are at the station relaxing, and on fiestas. The nature of these occasions controls the style of the interaction that accompanies them and forces the meeting of station and pueblo people into the public eye. Arguments, when they have taken place, have almost always been in the station bar, before a public jury. There is a conscious attempt to keep confrontations publicly visible.

The only recent trouble between the pueblo and an outsider, though it involved only a single person from the station barrio, points to the two communities' difference of interests and the inadequate definition of their respective responsibilities. The expropriation of land for the railroad made government property of land that would ordinarily be controlled by the común, if not by private owners. When one old track was abandoned and new ones laid, a no-man's-land came into existence. The railroad works foreman concentrates his crew's efforts on the new tracks and station. The old tracks and station are still theoretically under his jurisdiction, but he has not mobilized his crew for their upkeep, and they are falling into disuse. Pueblo shepherds pass through the area with their flocks. This fact was given tacit recognition in 1963 when the works foreman was invited to the San Antonio feast, representing the railroad in the ownership of stubble. In general, such things as abandoned furnishings from the old station were used with care "in the public good" in ways that concerned both communities—for instance, in the church or school.

In late 1965, when a dead tree toppled over by the old tracks, the vecinos had it sawed into planks which they planned to use in the construction of a shed to house the común's newly purchased thresher. When the planks arrived in the station to be picked up, the works foreman confronted the only vecino who was in the station at the time and informed him that the tree was really railroad property, had been illegally confiscated, and was not being used "in the public good." The ensuing loud argument aligned the foreman against the one vecino and the priest, who had appeared on the scene, and the foreman publicly named the alcalde as chief offender. The railroad community as a whole never entered the argument, but the foreman took it up as a personal cause. The común stood solidly behind its alcalde and the notion that a thresher shed was indeed in the public good, although the council immediately announced that the planks would be used in the schoolhouse instead.

Despite the announcement of the new use for the planks, the

foreman made a great deal of noise and some telephone calls, and he eventually presented the alcalde with a document showing that he (the foreman) was in charge of the unused railroad properties. The alcalde suggested that the state of the properties did not show that the foreman was taking his charge seriously and invited him to assume his responsibilities without delay. The foreman went off in a huff, to return later with a threat to collect rent on the lands in question from the común. The council met to agree on a rental rate in case the threat materialized: they agreed to pay the fixed price of stubble per hectare and to go no higher. But before the foreman took further steps, if he had ever intended to, he was transferred to a post in another province and the matter was laid to rest.

The alcalde, of course, was not responsible for the disposal of the disputed tree, for all such matters are decided upon by the council. The común thus faces its adversaries and handles their demands as a single, corporate personality. It is unable to control outsiders' behavior as it controls that of its own members, and it is usually forced into a purely defensive position, but it is able to meet challenges jointly. In this sense, as in others, the común is a mutual-aid society and a protective buffer for the individuals who compose it. The maintenance of good relations with the station barrio seems to hinge on the barrio's lack of internal organization and its disunity of interest, if not apathy. To more powerful voices or threats from outside its boundaries, the común bows, but its members bow together.

# Alliances

# 5

We're somewhat related to the widow Josefa, you see. Her grandmother was widowed and got remarried to my husband's mother's father, who was a widower in Salcedo. They were older when they married and they had no more children.

—A daughter of the pueblo

Marriage between natives of different villages and emigration create networks of kinship ties which, even in the absence of other ties, would give any family numerous contacts outside the común. In truth, outside contacts are hardly confined to kin groups, but the kinship networks form the springboard for the formation of other alliances.

In a variety of ways, tradition favors endogamous marriage. Throughout Spain, populations tend to be endogamous where their size permits. In the Sierra Ministra, there is a high percentage of endogamous couples in the larger towns, but the hamlets can hardly follow their example. Among some of Valdemora's neighbors, for instance, endogamous households in the común de vecinos number, in Mazarulleque 31 of 40 (77.5 percent), in Molinos 28 of 36 (77.8 percent), in Aguasalida 15 of 41 (36.6 percent), and in Salcedo 8 of 20 (40.0 percent), whereas in Valdemora only one of the living común couples is endogamous, and one of the two widows is a daughter of the pueblo who married a vecino—that is, 12.5 percent of the married vecinos and children of the pueblo in Valdemora are endogamous. This is about 16.7 percent of farmers' marriages. Endogamous matches even in small populations are often possible because consanguineal and affinal matches are not only permitted, but traditionally encouraged. The only forbidden matches are within the direct line and between siblings. Otherwise, with Church dispensation, cousins may marry, aunts and uncles may marry nephews and nieces, affines may marry, and ritual kin may marry.[1] Cousin marriage and the marriage of affines (pairs of siblings of two families and widowed people with deceased spouses' siblings) are particularly common. Of the seventy-five común marriages recorded in genealogies in 1963 for three generations of Valdemorans, fourteen (18.7 percent) were contracted between consanguineal or affinal relations: three were between first cousins, one between more distant cousins, six between groups of siblings, and three between widowed persons and siblings of their deceased spouses.

The explicit rationale behind cousin marriages and the duplication of marriage ties between two sibling groups is that property can thus be merged. Valdemorans now look down on these forms of marriage, which are contracted less often today than some decades ago, because they were usually arranged out of what are considered economic interests and were not based on mutual affection of the partners. Valdemorans today view the love-match as the only one which makes a happy home. Marriage of widowed people with their siblings-in-law is explicitly viewed as being for the benefit of the children—so that the children may be reared by a blood relation rather than by a strange step-parent. But these matches, too, are becoming less frequent, as is the death of young mothers in childbirth, which seems to have been the most frequent event causing men's remarriage. Nor are these matches admired, and they are often said to be bad rather than good for the children.

There is a strong tendency toward village endogamy quite apart from consanguineal and affinal marriages, and this is re-

1. Cf. Regatillo 1965, pp. 370 ff. Among affines, marriage in the direct line (for example, father-in-law with daughter-in-law) is rarely dispensable, but other affinal matches are quite easily contracted.

flected in the traditions of competition between mozo groups, in the exaction of fees from foreign mozos, and in customs such as that of San Juan, when girls with native novios are given flowers and those with foreign novios receive weeds or branches from the mozos of the pueblo.

Genealogies and other records yield interesting data on marriage patterns and especially on the effects of the railroad community on these patterns. First, a word of explanation on the use of the documents is in order. The data presented here on marriage and emigration are drawn almost exclusively from the genealogies of today's farmers. Genealogies were supplemented by information from church and other archives, but individuals known from documents alone were always noted separately. Such cases have extended the records of some families several generations beyond the earliest memories of the informants. However, documentary information is usually incomplete.[2] Sometimes there are data only on the people who remained in Valdemora as vecinos, with no data on their siblings. Where there are data on their siblings, it is often not known how many of them reached maturity, what marriages they contracted, or their places of residence. Thus, it is often impossible to distinguish between a case of infant mortality and a case of emigration. Because of these factors, I have hesitated to use documentary information where its inclusion causes loss of control of detail; thus the statistics on marriage and emigration are considered only for the three most recent generations: currently active vecinos form the base generation (Vec.), their parents' generation is the first ascending generation (A-1), and their children's generation the first filial generation (F-1). (The figure on the endsheets does not separate generations in the pueblo by

2. This is often due to the fact that some documents have been lost rather than to inadequate recording. Where church records are fully preserved, data are available on all births and baptisms in the parish, on all deaths of residents, and on the marriages of all who appear on the baptismal rolls. Data are lacking, however, on the deaths of emigrants and on places of residence of emigrants.

the same principles used in the marriage study: active vecinos do not fall into a single group on the endsheets figure.) There is an age range of about thirty years in each group, the three groups combined covering approximately one century. The F-1 group is, of course, still growing. Only half of the F-1 group was of marriageable age in 1963. A-1 marriages occurred between about 1887 and 1936, Vec. marriages between 1920 and 1959, and the first F-1 marriage took place in 1953.

The concentration on genealogical records requires some comment. The present and the very recent past composition of the community are fully documented. But genealogies collected in the field are subject to one condition which must be recognized, especially for a population from which there is consistent emigration. A family which emigrates totally, either en masse or by failing to produce male residents, might leave no trace for the fieldworker, though such a family was an integral part of the community a generation or two ago. A study based on genealogical information necessarily omits consideration of such cases and only through other records does these families' long-time status in the village become evident. The farther back the examination goes (Valdemorans seldom remember beyond the second ascending generation), the genealogies increasingly contain only a sample of the population. The question is whether this sample is representative of the total population—if those families whose lines are forgotten today left Valdemora in special circumstances or if their disappearance is part of a gradual process which occurs naturally in village history. Documentary sources support the latter assumption for the period of recorded history—since the late sixteenth century. First, there have been no significant fluctuations in population size since that time, and thus there has been no notable spurt in emigration (or mortality). Second, documents show a persistent pattern of continual emigration from all segments of the population.

It is clear from church records that in the normal functioning of the system, family lines have a definite life-span in Valdemora.

Both emigration and the birth of females cause surnames to die out in due course. No vecinos today bear the surnames of the vecinos of the 1750 cadaster, though they do bear some genealogical relationship to vecinos of 1750. Similarly, marriage records for the mid-sixteenth century do not contain surnames of vecinos of 1750, though the two populations were doubtless related at many points. The concentration of certain surnames is identified with certain towns in the area; for instance, the names of Gutierrez and Ocen are presently most concentrated in Valdemora. A survey of the documents indicates that these concentrations shift with time from one village to another. Valdemorans with the names of Antón and Alonso are all related to immigrants from Aguasalida families in the late eighteenth century. The Gonzalo family descends from an immigrant from a more distant Sierra village, and the youngest generation of Valdemora Gonzalos has already emigrated in its entirety, thus ending that family's life in the village. The Gutierrez family cannot be traced in Valdemora beyond the fourth ascending generation from the present vecinos; there are records of the Rangils only to the fifth ascending generation; and the Ocen family descends from an Aguasalida immigrant of the sixth ascending generation. Such records indicate that a family line rarely if ever achieves a life span in Valdemora of 200 years, but 150 years is not uncommon. At any given point in time, then, some families who can be known through documents and whom some informants also knew will not appear in genealogies. But the sample contained in genealogies can be used for any period in which supplementary documentation can illuminate the nature of the sample.

Both marriage and emigration statistics are considered for a population of necessarily arbitrary limits. I have included all individuals who are offspring of vecino families. People who immigrated to Valdemora from elsewhere as adults and became vecinos are not included, although their children are. Children who emigrated from Valdemora with their parents are not considered, though their parents are if they were of vecino families. The chief concern here is that all members of the population studied were raised from childhood in the Valdemora farm community. The marriage records thus reflect only the alliances of individuals who met their spouses in the context of village social life. Emigrants from the population thus delimited are not mere transients, but individuals who at one time had fixed roots in Valdemora. The population of Valdemora, thus defined, includes the farm community and totally excludes the railroad community, except where there is intermarriage between the two communities. The son of a vecino who does not farm, but works for the railroad, although he may live in Valdemora, is considered an emigrant, as is the vecino's daughter who marries a nonfarmer, though he, too, may be the son of a vecino. This definition of the community boundaries corresponds, with infrequent exceptions, to the way in which the común de vecinos traditionally defines itself.[3]

Genealogies indicate a diminishing frequency of marriages where both spouses are of the común: in the A-1 generation 16.7 percent of the marriages were común-endogamous, 10.0 percent in the Vec. generation, and none in the F-1 generation by 1967. Villagers are able to give supplementary data on all of the individuals involved in the marriage study—data on their occupations and the circumstances in which they met their spouses. Thus, many of the marriages involving one partner from outside the común can be shown to have been contracted solely in the context of village social life—that is, between children of the pueblo and individuals from families who were actually resident there either in railroad occupations or in related contexts. Thus the list of común-endogamous marriages may be supplemented by a list of territorially-endogamous marriages. The rate of "effective" endogamy combined with the rate of común endogamy yields a rate of total endogamy which, for the total population of the municipality, approximates the rate in larger villages (see table 4). It is evident

3. Household 12 on table 2, headed by the part-time farmer who did not enter the común, has been included in the analysis of marriage and emigration.

that the presence of the railroad and the additional population it supports have made it possible for Valdemorans to make matches without venturing far from home.

TABLE 4

Rates of Común Endogamy and Effective Endogamy in Valdemora Marriages

| Generation | Total Marriages | Endogamy Común | % | Effective | % | Total | % |
|---|---|---|---|---|---|---|---|
| A-1 | 30 | 5 | 16.7 | 3 | 10.0 | 8 | 26.7 |
| Vec. | 40 | 4 | 10.0 | 8 | 20.0 | 12 | 30.0 |
| F-1 (to 1967) | 9 | 0 | 00.0 | 2 | 22.2 | 2 | 22.2 |

It is interesting to compare the figures from table 4 with records of marriages predating the railroad era in Valdemora. I have records of ninety-seven marriages contracted between 1680 and 1875, the latter date being the earliest point at which Valdemorans would have felt the effects of a railroad population. These marriages are not included in the detailed study because they do not appear in genealogies, or in the relevant groups on the genealogies. It is possible, though, to estimate a rate of endogamy for the early period. Eighteen of the ninety-seven marriages recorded are endogamous, showing 18.6 percent común endogamy. This estimate is probably too high, as a number of marriages contracted by Valdemora males were probably recorded in the wives' towns, where weddings generally take place.[4] It is reasonable to assume, therefore, that the rate of común endogamy was not significantly higher than the 16.7 percent indicated for the A-1 generation by the more reliable data. This would support the suggestion that the railroad has indeed played an important role in enlarging the

4. These cases would ordinarily be recorded on the margins of the baptismal rolls in Valdemora. The baptismal rolls for most of this period are not preserved, however, and only their index remains, so that men's marriages with foreign women are not noted.

possibilities of mate selection in town. The trend in the F-1 group is still hard to discern; all but two of the marriages to date are with people from nearby towns.

The data on postmarital residence (table 5) show the traditional tendency toward residence in the husband's village when he farms land there. All five cases of común endogamy in the A-1 group involved farmers, and all five couples took up residence in Valdemora.

TABLE 5

Post-Marital Residence

| Generation | Residence | | |
|---|---|---|---|
| | Valdemora | Town of Foreign Spouse | Neolocal |
| A-1 couples | | | |
| Común endogamy | 5 | . . . | 0 |
| Husband Valdemoran | 6* | 3† | 3 |
| Wife Valdemoran | 2† | 6* | 5 |
| Vec. couples | | | |
| Común endogamy | 1 | . . . | 3 |
| Husband Valdemoran | 9* | 1† | 8 |
| Wife Valdemoran | 4†[a] | 3* | 11 |
| F-1 couples | | | |
| Común endogamy | 0 | . . . | 0 |
| Husband Valdemoran | 1* | 1† | 3 |
| Wife Valdemoran | 0† | 0* | 4 |

* Virilocal

† Uxorilocal

[a] All four cases are of women of vecino families married to men whose work keeps them in Valdemora. All four women have rented or sold most of their inherited land and are considered emigrants from the farm community.

All but one case of residence in the wife's village involved men who farmed their wives' holdings. Uxorilocal residence in Valdemora increased in the Vec. generation. This is due to several cases where the man is connected with the railroad and holds a salaried job, and some of these couples at the same time have access to the wives' vegetable gardens and urban property in Valdemora. In addition, in the Vec. group, only one of the four común-endogamous couples remained in Valdemora as farmers. The rest, though of farm families, established neolocal residence in larger towns, where the men held salaried jobs. The most striking change is occurring in the shift toward neolocality (usually in cities), which claimed 26.7 percent of A-1 couples, rose to 55.0 percent of Vec. couples, and may eventually claim almost all couples in the F-1 group, where by 1967 seven of the nine F-1 marriages were neolocal. The rising rate of neolocality is the strongest indicator of the type of emigration that is occurring: small farm communities are being forsaken altogether in favor of salaried jobs in the growing cities of the nation. None of the young girls in the village wants to marry a farmer. All instead look forward to an easier life in a town with at least one movie theater and a husband in a salaried position.

Marriages were traditionally contracted with families from villages within a fairly short radius of Valdemora. It is possible to plot on a map the home towns of individuals who married Valdemorans before 1875—that is, before the railroad might have extended villagers' contacts. In order to consider the broadest possible area, I included twenty-one marriages contracted between 1581 and 1679 which are not completely enough documented for use in any other part of the study, in addition to the ninety-seven better-documented marriages that were used to estimate the rate of común endogamy before 1875. The great majority of towns falls within a sixteen-kilometer radius of Valdemora, as the crow flies (no more than a day's walk by the paths), and none lies farther than thirty-six kilometers away in a straight line. It is particularly instructive to compare more recent marriages against the map drawn for 1581–1875. In the A-1 generation, only two of the thirty marriages involve people from outside a radius of forty kilometers from Valdemora: a Valdemora man married a French woman, and a Valdemora woman married a Galician. In the Vec. generation, seven out of forty marriages were contracted outside a forty-kilometer radius. Four of these marriages are with people from more distant towns within the province and three are with people from more distant provinces. Of the five F-1 marriages contracted by 1963, three are with people from elsewhere in the province and two with people from Barcelona. Since 1963, three F-1 marriages contracted are with people from neighboring towns and a fourth with a resident of the same province. It is interesting that two-thirds of all Valdemora marriages since 1940 can be plotted within the same forty-kilometer radius which determined the range for the mid-sixteenth to the mid-nineteenth centuries.

Documents suggest that the range of contact of other small villages in the area is similar to that of Valdemora. Salcedo, for example, has had more sustained contact with some villages a bit farther north of the area covered by a sixteen-kilometer radius from Valdemora, but, being such close neighbors, the contacts of the two towns have been largely the same. The farther two towns lie from one another, the fewer common contacts they may be expected to have had. The data on larger villages suggest that, with more endogamy, their outside contacts through intermarriage are not necessarily more frequent or any more extensive than those of their smaller neighbors.

We can now draw a much clearer picture of the way in which the traditional social life functions. I have mentioned the visiting pattern connected with fiestas. Such visiting is largely between members of the bilateral, extended family. The emigration of almost all females at marriage and of some males gives every Valdemora family contacts in nearby towns. A young brother and sister from Valdemora stay with an aunt in Salcedo for a fiesta, with an older sister in Medinaceli for a celebration there, and again with another aunt in Pedrosa for that town's saint's day. The young man may meet a girl from Aguasalida who is also staying with an aunt in Salcedo, and they may renew their acquaintance at the next fiesta in Valdemora, eventually marrying and settling there. The young man's sister may marry a farmer in Pedrosa and become the second member of the family to settle there. Relatives of her Aguasalida sister-in-law may become new visitors to Pedrosa, where they have not previously had much contact.

There is a tendency for families to establish multiple connections in certain other towns. Here, consanguineal and affinal marriages have played an important role in binding two families by more than one tie. Even without these forms of marriage, the visiting pattern fosters marriages in towns where some connection has already been established. Valdemora genealogies show some families with multiple connections in one part of the map, some with a concentration of contacts in another part. The children of Valdemorans in other towns will, of course, assume contacts in a sphere different from Valdemora's own. Thus, the area as a whole may be viewed as a series of overlapping networks of intervillage ties through which the identities of family lines shift, over the generations, from one village to another, gradually shedding the more ancient connections and continually assuming new ones.

Kinship networks outside Valdemora are not based on intervillage marriage alone, for emigration is responsible for much of their extension. The emigration of females at marriage, and occasionally of male farmers who establish uxorilocal residence, accounts for most of the demographic movement between farm villages. But this part of Castile has long been noted for occupational movement as well, which ordinarily takes people away from the farm villages. The province of Soria, for example, has traditionally sent many people into several migratory or semimigratory occupations—as teamsters, as transhumant shepherds, or as foremen in the olive presses of Andalusia.[5] These migrations are well documented for the later Middle Ages and were tightly organized by the relevant guilds (the Royal Mesta among them, of course). In Jaen and Seville, groups of Sorians have maintained

5. Tudela 1949; the province of Soria is better studied in this respect than is Guadalajara.

their identity, some with an occupational identity as well, such as the textile workers in Seville.[6] Tudela notes the existence of Sorian populations in Cádiz as well as Seville—people originally of pastoral occupations who settled in the south and entered commercial life.[7] These people maintained strong provincial identity, and they were organized and commercially quite powerful in the eighteenth century. A form of temporary migration of females is also old in the Sierra Ministra. In families with many children, older daughters would be sent out, either as domestics in private families or to kinsmen who had fewer children. Their tour of duty ended either when they married or when their own families had fewer mouths to feed. Today, families are smaller and this particular form of female emigration has almost disappeared. But some of the older women in the villages, as a result of having been farmed out as girls, are familiar with a greater variety of life-styles than are the men, and some of them are widely traveled.

The frontiers of the New World claimed some migrants from the Sierra Ministra, but seemingly fewer than from areas of greater inequality in land ownership. There are Sorian populations, however, in Buenos Aires, in the textile trade, and in Vera Cruz, Mexico. Today, Valdemoran genealogies show very little movement to the New World.[8]

The priesthood and military establishment in Spain have been important places of employment for "extra" sons. Again, there is little evidence that these have been outlets for Valdemorans. Genealogies yield no record of any members of the clergy or career officers in military service. Rather, these seem to have been greater outlets for the upper classes.

Finally, the Sierra villages near Valdemora do not participate

6. Julio González, personal communication.

7. Tudela 1949.

8. Genealogies actually give a sampling from numerous Sierra villages, since complete genealogies were recorded for all of the women married into the común.

notably in the labor migrations to other parts of Europe, which must be reckoned as a major force elsewhere in the nation.[9] Instead, the vast majority of Sierra emigrants today are moving into Spanish cities.

Table 6 shows the number of surviving offspring in each of the three generations studied and the number of emigrants of each sex. That there is a high rate of emigration in the total population

TABLE 6

Emigration from Valdemora

| Generation | Surviving Offspring | Emigrants |
|---|---|---|
| A-1 | | |
| Male | 21 | 10 (47.6%) |
| Female | 22 | 16 (72.7%) |
| Total | 43 | 26 (60.5%) |
| Vec. | | |
| Male | 26 | 13 (50.0%) |
| Female | 22 | 21 (95.5%) |
| Total | 48 | 34 (70.8%) |
| F-1[a] | | |
| Male | 19 | 8 (42.1%) |
| Female | 11 | 4 (36.4%) |
| Total | 30 | 12 (40.0%) |

[a] To 1963.

is borne out by the figures for the A-1 and Vec. generations. The exact frequency of emigration cannot be documented for earlier periods, but the very nature of the documentary evidence points overwhelmingly to a frequency of over 50 percent, but less than 75 percent, of the total population in each generation. That is, genealogies and various other documents usually yield information regarding only one male, occasionally two, and a few females, from the range of children whom we know from church records

9. Some southern communities from which there is heavy European migration are currently under study by David Gregory of the Department of Anthropology, University of Pittsburgh.

to have been born to given parents. All of the other siblings cannot possibly be accounted for by mortality alone, and thus some must have emigrated. Informants frequently remember that their great-grandfathers resided in Valdemora, but they do not recall the existence of a great-grandfather's brother, probably because he emigrated from the town. The great-grandfather may appear in the genealogy, although his brother does not: thus the actual number of emigrants in early generations cannot be divined, but it must be assumed that it was considerable.

In the A-1 and Vec. groups, about half of the male population emigrated. Not all of the F-1 group has reached the age of decision regarding occupation, residence, and marital status. (The high proportion of males in this group is the result of four female deaths in one family.) In 1963, eleven of the thirty F-1 individuals had made this decision. By 1967, the future of several others was becoming increasingly clear. Only one man in the F-1 group has cast his lot as a farmer. The young F-1 farmer married in December 1967 and brought his wife into the común. Everyone felt that he would be the last man to establish a new household in the común. Younger males were already preparing to leave town. One family, Household 12, emigrated in its entirety in 1965: the part-time postal employee took a full-time postal job in Pamplona and left his holding in rent with his brothers, moving from Valdemora with his wife and three young sons. Four boys from three other households had been sent away by 1967 to complete their secondary education. Two slightly older boys—one of whom had been farming with his father—got postal jobs in Pamplona through their former neighbor.[10] Thus, there remained in the común only two boys, one under age ten and the other an infant, four girls who were still in school (that is, under age fourteen), and three older girls who worked with their mothers at home. It is probable that only the two F-1 males already mentioned will not emigrate and that virtually all of the females will do so at marriage.

10. One of these boys returned in 1968 to a postal job in Valdemora, but his future as a part-time farmer is uncertain.

Thus, we can reasonably project a figure of 85 percent male emigration in the F-1 group, a drastic increase over previous generations, indicative of a real change in village life. This trend is already reflected in the increased rate of neolocality.

During the period covered by the genealogies, the population of Spanish cities has grown steadily. A comparison of the 1901 and 1960 populations of several major cities shows that they have at least doubled in size, if not tripled, in that period: Barcelona grew from 533,000 to 1,503,062; Bilbao from 83,306 to 267,293; Madrid from 539,855 to 1,966,070; Málaga from 130,109 to 318,102; Seville from 148,315 to 450,213; Valencia from 213,550 to 571,452; and Zaragoza from 99,118 to 299,181.[11] This trend is well attested by the number of Valdemora emigrants who have moved to larger towns and nonfarm jobs (see table 7). Emigration to other farms has decreased steadily since the A-1 generation. In the Vec. generation, the number of emigrants who either remained

TABLE 7

Residence of Emigrants From Valdemora

| Generation | Total Emigrants | Residence: Farms | Small-Town (nonfarm) | Urban |
|---|---|---|---|---|
| A-1 | 26 | 6 | 0 | 20 (76.9%)[a] |
| Vec. | 34 | 2 | 6 | 26 (76.5%) |
| F-1[b] | 12 | 0 | 1 | 11 (91.7%) |

[a] One group of eight siblings emigrated as a unit to South America.
[b] To 1963.

in Valdemora or emigrated to nearby small towns in nonfarm jobs increased, for this was a period of considerable railroad construction. But by far the largest proportion of emigrants has moved into more urban situations. The urban segments of families' kinship networks are acquiring increasing importance in village life.

11. Nuevo atlas de España 1961, p. 145.

Obviously, they extend the range and types of people's contacts far beyond the range and types produced by intervillage marriage alone.

Kinship networks are very extensive quite apart from their spread into urban areas. As mentioned earlier, any individual is "somewhat related" to a great number of other people. The bilateral reckoning of kinship accounts for only part of the extension of ties. The number of possible ties is further extended by the facts that there are no recognized limits to relatedness and that affines are as much a part of a person's network as are his blood relations. Mourning for affines and the requirement of dispensation for affinal marriages reflect the degree to which the married couple becomes a single unit with respect to the kinsmen of both partners. In practice, people are careless in distinguishing affines from blood relations, among close as well as distant relations (except in the case of step-parents), and for activating contacts outside the común there may be literally a score of ways of claiming relationship with a family in another village. The choice of the way in which ties are claimed may vary with the demands of different situations and with sentiment. And, as I have said, whether two people claim relationship at all often depends upon the immediate social context. Two común families may deny common ties in daily affairs, while claiming extensive ties outside the común, but when the común is active as a unit, all members are considered to be as closely related as any of them is to outsiders. The manner of reckoning relationship between blocs of families is, as I have said, the same in both contexts.

Marriage patterns seem to indicate the radius within which, by existing means of communication, the most active social life was traditionally carried on, but this radius does not circumscribe the extension of kinship networks, which are much more farflung. A Valdemoran with an aunt married to a vecino of Medinaceli might acquire many contacts through the aunt's husband, and their extension is hardly reflected in the simple record of a Valdemora-

Medinaceli marriage. But as a general rule, the geographically more farflung contacts are more difficult to maintain for daily purposes, so that much activity falls back into the close sphere in which contacts are sustained enough to continue producing intermarriages.

Networks of friendship are grafted on to those of kinship to extend them further: "my cousin in Salcedo knows a man who . . . ," or "the blacksmith in my uncle's pueblo is a good one for that. . . ." Most friends and acquaintances are identified with reference to someone in the kinship network. It is usually only within the territorial entity—including the station barrio—that a person might say of another, "we are friends," without specifying any other form of linkage.

Ritual kinship—those ties established between godparents, their godchildren, and the godchildren's parents—as it is contracted in Valdemora does not foster the creation of new alliances between families as it tends to do in some areas.[12] Instead, Valdemorans most frequently utilize existing contacts within the bilateral kinship network for the selection of godparents *(padrinos)* for baptisms and weddings. For their wedding, couples often select one godparent from the groom's family and the other from the bride's, but no strict pattern is followed. The godparent of either sex may come from either side, and sometimes both come from one side. Wedding godparents are almost invariably siblings or siblings-in-law of the new couple. There is some tendency to ask the wedding godparents to serve in the same capacity for the baptism of the couple's first child. This is by no means standard practice, but if a couple wishes to follow this rule and the wedding godparents are not available, stand-in godparents may serve in their stead and the names of the wedding godparents are officially inscribed on the church rolls. Each succeeding child is likely to have a separate set of godparents. Baptismal godparents again are generally

12. Cf. Pitt-Rivers 1958, 1961; Foster 1960. The term *compadre*, stressing the ties between the adults in the contract, is not in use in Valdemora.

siblings or other collateral kinsmen of the child's parents, but there is considerable variation here and the parents' nieces or nephews, their aunts or uncles, or even family friends may be asked to serve. There is sometimes a disparity in the ages of the two godparents and in their relationships to the child's family. I have been asked to serve myself, but could not as a non-Catholic, and the discovery of this restriction rather surprised the people who had asked me.

The casualness of the selection of godparents is understandable, since the baptismal godparents are not conceived as having a lasting relationship with their godchild as his padrinos or with the child's parents. Rather, their role as padrinos is usually subsumed by their role as kinsmen. A minor who is orphaned is legally the ward of his baptismal godparents only if no kinsman assumes this duty; the frequent selection of kinsmen as godparents thus redoubles the obligation of guardianship, while the selection of non-kin as godparents does not negate the recognized obligation of a child's kinsmen to serve as his guardian in any case. The most striking evidence for the casualness of the alliance is that parents cannot even recall the identity of the godfather in about 60 percent of the baptisms we discussed. One mother could not remember who had been the godfather of her youngest child, though the child was still less than two years old. The godmother is better remembered, for it is she who carries the child to church and holds it during the ceremony.[13] Couples are usually better at naming their

13. In Valdemora, a mother does not enter the church for forty days after giving birth and thus does not attend her children's baptisms. Valdemorans regard this as a Church rule, which it is not, though its biblical basis is clear (*Leviticus* 12 and *Luke* 2:22). There is evidence that the custom is not uncommon in Spain, but that it is disappearing. On the Santander-Burgos border, for instance, it is recognized as an old-fashioned practice, and modern mothers see their children baptized. Rev. Joaquín González Echegaray, an ethnohistorian of northern Spain, suggests that the one-time distribution of the practice and Church views of it have been little studied (personal communication). Oddly, the Holy Office of the Inquisition listed this among the practices which would help identify secret Judaizers (cf. Caro Baroja 1961, vol. 1, plate 84). This suggests that at least some-

wedding godparents, and weddings are much more memorable family events than are baptisms.

The godparents of confirmation, whenever this event occurs, serve for the entire group being confirmed and have no duties at all beyond the hour of the mass. The last time the bishop performed the confirmation in Valdemora, the alcalde and his wife served in this capacity.

Another even more casual relationship, but one which is given formal recognition at the time of baptism, is that of the child's family with the woman who attended the birth. There are no women in the village who consider themselves or are considered to be midwives, but any woman who has borne her own children might assist another in labor and childbirth. A few women who are considered more experienced are the most frequent attendants at births. They are said to "catch" or "gather up" babies *(recoger niños)*. Most births are attended by one of these women and by close female kin and the husband, unless the Medinaceli doctor feels that he will be needed. No Valdemora woman has, to my knowledge, given birth in a hospital, nor do I recall a case which the doctor attended. The neighbor who "catches" the baby is almost always invited to the baptismal ceremony and to the family party afterwards. Children and parents are all more apt to remember who "caught" each of the family's children than who their godfathers were, but the relationship is entirely a casual one. Far from being a paid service, assistance at the childbed is seen as a friendly service rendered by a neighbor.

That none of the relations of ritual kinship or assistance at childbirth are in themselves important and lasting alliances speaks for the adequacy of kin-based networks in filling the need for alliances without supplementation. It is possible that very highly endogamous yet occupationally homogeneous communities, such as exist on the high meseta of western Spain, might have greater

---

times, in some places, or for some purposes the forty-day rule has been formally viewed as an aberration.

reason to form special alliances with non-kin and specifically outside the village.[14]

In Valdemora, aside from those alliances contracted by the común as a body—formerly with the teacher and others—and today by all members with such public servants as the teacher, the priest, and the doctor, most of a family's needs can be met through kin-based contacts.[15] The only contacts which are sometimes based on independent considerations are the family's economic contacts with certain key figures: merchants, millers, blacksmiths, and stockmen. Here, economic considerations govern people's choices of whom to patronize, but once these decisions are made, the ties lead to personal acquaintanceship and become hard to break, even should the economic advantage seem to diminish. So it is that families tend to patronize certain businessmen rather than others over the years. These relationships may often originate independently of the kin-based networks and then become part of them, for people pass on information about their favored places of business to their kin and friends, and their favored businessmen have *become* their friends. A function of this system is, of course, that the steady customer will receive better service and other nonmaterial benefits. He repays special consideration primarily by assuming the task of advertising for the business, and this is important, for advertising is otherwise almost totally undeveloped. The world of economic transactions is an intensely personal one, and it is very rare in a villager's life that he should enter a place of business or deal with an individual utterly strange to him. Even in Madrid, visiting Valdemorans do not usually enter stores or bars which are strange to both them and their kinsmen.

14. Campbell (1964) documents a very clear case for the Sarakatsani of Greece. The Andalusian town studied by Pitt-Rivers (1961), though more heterogeneous internally, appears to have tendencies in this direction. Some important regions of Spain are unexplored from this point of view.

15. On the roles of brokers, intermediaries, patrons, etc., cf. the analyses of Wolf 1956, Geertz 1960, Kenny 1960, Foster 1963, Campbell 1964, Silverman 1965.

Itinerant tradesmen, whom an individual cannot really select, may be denied patronage in favor of a known competitor nearby. For example, a cheese-maker comes through Valdemora each year, selling his services along with the milk of his goats. Many people patronize him, but if they prefer not to, the same kind of cheese can be obtained at several places in Sigüenza. If itinerant stockmen do not offer a satisfactory price on young lambs or on aging sheep, a farmer goes to a livestock market to sell instead. Farmers know of several itinerant groups of shearers and can contract with whichever ones they choose at shearing time. The same holds for the purchase of farm equipment, the sale of wax and honey, the sale of wool, and so on. But in some cases, itinerant tradesmen allow farmers an occasional escape from the personal pressures of their ordinary dealings. The only instances in which people have little choice are in purchasing fresh bread, fresh milk, and fresh meat and fish. Here they are dependent upon one baker, one cow owner, two fishmongers, and one butcher daily. When they are shopping, women's complaints about prices (which are not normally subject to haggling) are in inverse proportion to the freedom they have in choosing their merchants. In a family's most important transaction of all, the sale of surplus wheat, the only buyer is the government wheat service, and the price is fixed, so on this subject the complaining is eternal.

The amorphous networks described here form the basis for the exchange of certain goods and services as well as for the spread of information of all kinds and for visiting. I have said that there is some exchange of regional specialities among kinsmen. Services as well are involved. For example, most emigrants to lower altitudes have their hams cured in Valdemora, by their families, for the alleged superior results. They, in turn, do varieties of errands for their village kin, especially if they travel in from urban centers.

Within the farm villages, it is kinsmen and friends, rather than neighbors, who form what cooperative farm labor groups there are. People who are relatively free at the time may go to a kinsman's village to help out during the weeks of weeding, harvesting, or threshing. Families arrange dates for the sheep shearing and the pig slaughter so that they may be free to assist each other then. Común families, who do not help each other in the pig slaughter, sometimes help or receive assistance from families in the station barrio with whom they are friendly. The dependence upon close kinsmen or outsiders in these things is absolute; neighbors do not render these services to one another merely on the basis of común membership. The lending of tools and equipment is largely between kinsmen and close friends, sometimes regardless of distance. Even people with close collateral kin in the común seem to prefer to give and seek help from outsiders instead. The only notable cooperation in the común is between parents and married children's households, for they are after all working for the same estate.[16] One daughter of the pueblo who generally has no time to put up blood sausages offers the blood and intestine to one very close friend only (and not to her kinsmen in the común) and throws them out if that family cannot use them: she says that others would interpret the offer as a form of charity and take offense. One vecino, when he was widowed in 1967, refused the offers of help from at least one común kinswoman and took all of his laundry to a sister-in-law in Aguasalida. In 1963, when his wife was already ill, this same man was the only vecino to harvest a full-scale holding by hand, though his kinsmen in the común had machinery; when these kinsmen joined a group to purchase a tractor, he was not included, though he said later that he would have joined them if he had been asked.

Perhaps the most striking feature of the networks is the way in which they are used for complementary purposes by villagers and their kinsmen who have emigrated to urban areas. The villager utilizes his urban contacts for visiting on special occasions; the pattern of intervillage visiting is simply extended to include urban neighborhoods in Madrid, Zaragoza, or Barcelona—the

16. The exceptions are the kinds of corporate groups which are now beginning to form for purposes of cooperative, mechanized farming (see chap. 6).

capitals which loom largest in Valdemora's social life. More important, the pattern of a family's urban contacts tends to determine the pattern of further emigration. A man with a large number of kinsmen in Barcelona is likely to look to Barcelona if he decides to emigrate or to help his children emigrate. At this point, the Barcelona kinsmen help to seek out employment and make arrangements for the newcomer's residence. A single person and usually even newly-emigrated couples almost invariably live with kin, paying them for room and board. The married couple finds its own apartment as soon as possible, but single people usually stay indefinitely with their relatives. People who so assiduously avoid co-residence in the village may feel considerable pressure in the more cramped circumstances of urban life, but the alternative of living alone is never considered. As a result of their initial co-residence, emigrants from specific regions tend to cluster together in certain neighborhoods. For example, Valdemoran genealogies show high concentrations of emigrants living in the outlying communities of Villaverde and Vallecas in Madrid and Hospitalet in Barcelona. The data on occupation show that Valdemorans' railroad contacts at home have been extremely important in employing emigrants away from the village. The postal service has played a smaller role in this respect. The rest of the occupational scene is dominated by factory and other blue-collar jobs. Only now are village boys beginning to receive vocational training which gives them access to higher paying jobs. One of the coveted positions for married emigrants with families is that of a building concierge, for this includes living quarters and allows even the husband to work some hours at a second job as well.

Unmarried women generally do not leave the village to find employment; they usually form part of the female work force at home. The exceptions are the mozas who leave town, sometimes only seasonally, to work as domestics, either in private families or in hotels. Again, they serve as contacts for other village girls who wish the same work. They are by no means real emigrants and are still working for their families at home.

Whereas villagers achieve routes to the outside via their emigrant relatives, emigrants appear to use contacts in the villages in order to remain part of the active social life there. A village or family fiesta—or sometimes just a Sunday—brings into Valdemora every emigrant who can possibly make the trip. Their life in the city does not offer them the same personal involvement in fiestas, and the desire to return to the village is marked even among emigrants' children who have not grown up there. The genealogies offer some details on the extent to which emigrants depend upon the village for part of their social life. Of the eighteen marriages contracted by emigrants of the A-1 generation, sixteen are with partners from towns within the traditional marriage radius (forty kilometers) which I have described (and of which the Valdemora railroad community is considered a part). Of the twenty-three marriages of Vec. generation emigrants, twenty-one are with partners from towns within the same area. Six of the nine F-1 marriages to date also fall within the forty-kilometer radius. Thus, in the older generations for which there is better information, when emigration was not postmarital (as it generally is for women), emigrants continued to have significant contacts in the contexts of village life.

Genealogies also yield information on the first generation of children growing up away from Valdemora—offspring of A-1 and Vec. generation parents who emigrated to points outside the traditional marriage radius. Of thirty-seven marriages contracted by these individuals, ten remain in the traditional range and eleven fall outside of it. My informants were unable to specify the home towns of the spouses in sixteen of the marriages, which in itself indicates that ties have loosened. There are few data on the children of these marriages, and many of them are not yet of marriageable age. There is apparently a further loss of contact in this, the second generation growing up away from the village. However, ten of thirty-seven marriages within the old radius is no small proportion for the children of emigrants and shows that considerable contact was maintained with the home village.

Emigrant families may be said to go through a period of adjustment in which the village offers them a social life which they still have not found in the city. The period of greatest contact with the village corresponds roughly with the years during which an emigrant retains legal control over his inherited lands. Ties loosen when lands are sold back to the members of the family who farm it. In most cases, the sale takes place before the second generation comes into its inheritance, but still some years after the owners have emigrated. Emigrants feel security in land ownership and in being able to collect rents in grain if they wish, as well as in being able to return to the village for social reasons. There is always the feeling that, if their new occupations fail, they have something to fall back on. While, as I have said, it is rarely possible for more than one heir to live successfully off an estate, the nonfarmer's security in retaining title to his holding is not a mere fiction: the yearly rents on one's share are usually equivalent to a year's supply of bread for a family of four or five. Farmers favor their emigrant kin with a special rental arrangement. When no other arrangement is agreed upon by the parties, and when rental rates are fixed in terms of wheat rather than cash, law permits the renter to pay the owner no more than half of the price which that amount of wheat would bring from the government warehouses. Kinsmen do not normally draw up formal leases, and rental within families is customarily at a rate of one fanega of wheat per fanega of land; thus village rentals are usually subject to the stipulated 50 percent reduction. It is usually understood among close kinsmen, however, that a farmer will pay his rent to them at the full market price of the wheat. The arrangement thus gives emigrants a fairly good potential bread supply. That this is a vital part of an emigrant's security seems well recognized on both sides. Another legal aspect of the rental arrangement assures that the village farm lands will not be dispersed among outsiders: an absentee owner cannot withdraw land from a tenant unless it is to work the land himself, and he cannot choose to sell land without giving the tenant first option on it. When an emigrant feels secure in his new environment, his holding almost inevitably reverts to his farmer kin or—in a rare case where the farmer does not choose to buy—to another vecino of the village.

The railroad has played a crucial role in facilitating communication between villages, and between the Sierra and the capital cities, and in extending the area over which people can have active contact with one another. According to the widow Josefa, vecinos were traveling by rail as soon as the service began. Although few of the villages have stations, key towns are served, and the access to Sigüenza, to provincial capitals of the Sierra provinces, and to Madrid, Zaragoza, and Barcelona are of prime importance. The roads have played a lesser part in communication, for even today most farmers do not own vehicles. Men sometimes use bicycles between villages lying in the same valley; recently a few mozos have acquired motorscooters; but I do not know of a single full-time farmer in the Sierra who owns a car, though two or three of the local tradesmen have bought them since 1964. The majority of farmers still do not own tractors, and those who do have not really extended their range of local travel by that means. The train is by far the most rapid and the cheapest means of travel at hand.

The railroad is the means for extending contacts in the social life, and the railroad personnel have vastly augmented the ranks of the intermediaries themselves. Train personnel in particular (as opposed to station personnel) act as all-purpose bearers between station towns. Every variety of message and parcel—clothing, medicines, foodstuffs, and miscellany—travel the railroad without their owners, guided from place to place by train personnel doing favors for their friends along the route. Thus, the farmer can do considerable shopping without leaving the village; this is where friendships in the station barrio prove valuable. Merchants on the one end and their clients on the other all make extensive use of the railroad in this way.

So far, I have not discussed villagers' relations with people who are in any sense specialized "brokers," people who can give villagers access to information, facilities, or contacts which are not otherwise available to them. On the village scene itself these are very few and their roles are quite limited. Most of the tradesmen and the secretary of the ayuntamiento scarcely merit mention outside of their inclusion in the general networks we have already discussed. Such people as butchers, the baker, or fruit dealers do not really have special functions in the social life. The priest, the doctor, and the school teacher, on the other hand, are viewed as specialists of one kind or another with knowledge and connections which set them apart. Of these, the priest is the only full-time resident of the village, and the doctor is not a resident at all. The teacher is, in my experience in the village, the least important of the three. In my years in Valdemora there has been continual difficulty in contracting a permanent teacher and holding her there. The hamlets are undesirable locations, as most teachers prefer larger towns, and their tendency is to leave the village for more attractive centers at every free moment; some even commute from outside. Many teachers are young women who, far from being regarded as real specialists, are seen simply as girls who have had a few years of extra schooling and will eventually marry and become housewives: the villagers' tendency is to protect them as single girls away from home, rather than to seek from them worldly advice, which they are hardly believed capable of rendering. Their opinions are sought only with respect to the children's schoolwork, but here their word carries considerable weight.

The priest's major duty aside from the offering of religious services is also in the realm of education. He is much more respected in his role in preparing children for their first communion and in offering advice on secondary schools outside the village than for his attempted moral instruction of the adult community, which does not find him equal to that task. He is considered eminently competent in teaching children, for he has had book-learning, and this he is expected to pass on. But no Valdemoran believes that book-learning necessarily imparts moral stature, and the entire community actively denies the priest real leadership.

The doctor is better liked than the priest, perhaps because he lives elsewhere, but the extent of his brokerage is also very limited: medical advice only is sought from him, nor are villagers able to have much casual contact with him, since he serves many villages and calls in each only where he is needed.

The striking aspect of Valdemorans' relations with the specialists who serve them is that the community as a whole, almost as a matter of explicit policy, denies these people any but their professional roles. It is a community, typical in the Sierra Ministra, which does not allow people to assume the multi-functional role of the patron or allow the emergence of the political bosses, or *caciques*, who achieve power in other communities. Within the village, there is no mandate for power: the farmer himself has no basis for the achievement of power; outsiders are granted occupational status and personal prestige, but the village yields nothing to personal ambition and forces its expression into arenas outside the village. That much of this quality may derive from Valdemora's lack of economic stratification has already been suggested, but much also owes to the strength of the horizontal principle of organization in the public aspects of village life. The modes of organization described in chapters 2 and 4, and the sanctions which encourage their persistence, make of the vecinos a corporate body which permits no personal manipulation from within and fights intrusions from without. At the same time, the great extension of personal contact networks allows villagers to seek elsewhere the things for which they might otherwise depend upon local patrons. Significantly, the only person in Valdemora who enjoys the position of a multi-purpose broker is neither an outsider nor professionally educated, and he is important, not because of his social status, but because he is the agent through whom people can vastly extend their personal contacts: he is the station restaurateur and he is to the village the embodiment of what the railroad itself is.

Ambrosio Tamayo, called simply Tamayo, was the son of a vecino of Calzada who retired from farming to keep a small general store in Valdemora, where his children in part grew up. The father was given the station bar-restaurant concession near the end of his life, at the retirement of the family who then held it, and at the senior Tamayo's death the RENFE granted the concession to the son, the present holder. Tamayo's succession came in the year of his marriage to the daughter of a Valdemora vecino. Some of his importance as a broker is doubtless due to the length of his tenure in the job—now over twenty-five years—but much also to the fact that he has never been a foreigner to the people of the surrounding villages, so that his ties in the Sierra are even older than the ones he has built up with railroad personnel and tradesmen in the region. Because he feeds both railroad personnel and passengers, he must deal with many more merchants—for foodstuffs, supplies, and equipment—than serve Valdemora. The railroad and the telephone are his instruments of transaction, and his agents include railroad personnel who service major centers from Madrid to Barcelona and north to the Pyrenees. A farmer, who does not necessarily know many train personnel himself, can make contact through Tamayo, who has old friends among conductors, engineers, and traveling officials of all sorts. If errands are important, Tamayo imposes upon his friends and one day returns the favor. Similarly, Tamayo is an important client of business concerns in many cities and he can connect a needy friend with someone whom he might otherwise never have known of. Further, Tamayo as a matter of course imports luxury goods which few other Sierra merchants carry and is one of the few in the Sierra whose scale of operation permits him the active philosophy that the customer is always right. Since he conceives of himself as—and indeed is—a public servant, Tamayo refuses no one his services. In this sense, he is anything but a patron in the village, for he serves all equally, though he, like everybody else, has special friends with whom he exchanges special favors. But, again, all of his relationships are conceived to be symmetrical ones between social equals, be they with farmers, railroad people, or merchants. This is true of all of the relationships within networks which I have described so far (except for the cases of the doctor, priest, and teacher), and these are all symmetrical relationships involving the exchange of similar goods and services from both sides.

This brings us to the issues of villagers' relationships with people who are by any reckoning their social superiors rather than their equals: these are the asymmetrical, dyadic, informally contracted, and multi-purpose patron-client relationships.[17] Valdemora, like other Sierra villages, by virtue of its lack of social stratification, is not a setting in which patron-client relationships form. Further, the extensive contact networks with good communications within them serve many of the same ends we might expect patronage to serve.[18] On the whole, patronage plays a very small part in the villagers' lives. Although the institution has been regarded as pervasive in Spain, it must be sought in more stratified communities. There are in reality few needs which a Valdemora farmer cannot fill otherwise. Emigrants to more heterogeneous centers, however, move into the patronage system. The only way in which Valdemorans seem to use the system is through their emigrant kinsmen. The most frequent manifestation is probably when villagers ask their relatives outside the village to help them find jobs, and the latter turn to their own employers in their search for possibilities.

There are respects in which the común as a body feels the need of the kinds of connections which patronage gives, as in its current dealings with the House of Medinaceli (see chapter 6), but the contacts are entirely lacking. Individual families simply seek help outside the pueblo; the común is unable to do this without relinquishing its corporate identity for that of a mere aggregate of people with different outside ties. The común deals as a body only with those individuals or institutions which deal with it as a body, and this limits the horizon significantly. It is far from certain if, in a previous era, the House of Medinaceli acted as a patron to

17. Cf. Kenny 1960, Foster 1963, Campbell 1964, Silverman 1965.

18. Silverman (1965) documents a shift away from patronage institutions with improved communications and modernization in central Italy.

the villages under its jurisdiction. The nature of the feudal regime in this area was far from the classic type which reigned in central Europe and England; the lord and the villagers were not in daily contact, and it seems to have been the común, rather than individuals, that dealt directly with the Church and the Duchy. If there was anything resembling the manor, it was to be found only in Medinaceli. It is likely that village priests, rather than the Medinaceli family, were the peasants' real contacts with the larger system. In addition to the priests, we know from the cadaster of 1750 that some noblemen had estates and maintained houses in the villages, even though they resided elsewhere most of the time: there is record of the estate of one Marqués in Valdemora, a resident of Soria, and also of one or two *hidalgos* (descendents, often illegitimate, of noble families) who farmed in the pueblo. Documents give no hint of their relationships with the common vecinos other than that they sometimes rented plots to farmers. However, the farmer most frequently rented directly from the Church or from a chaplaincy left to it and thus, again, had more dealings with Church powers than with secular ones.

In one other respect, also now obsolete, farmers may have had relations with families of higher social status—that is, with families who employed village girls in their homes. Since distance separated them, their contact was probably infrequent and hardly casual, but it is possible that such families once served farmers as patrons in some contexts. Today, we must conclude that patronage is but a very small part of the spectrum of a family's alliances outside the común, nor do we have the data to show that it was formerly much more important. We know, however, that kin-based networks of alliances are as old as is the fact of intervillage marriage itself, and that the dispersion of craftsmen and other specialists throughout the Sierra is also an old phenomenon, and to these we must assign primary social importance.

# 6 Change I: The Común and Family Estates

> If I'm in a little cooperative, I'm likely to quarrel with the few other people in it with me. If I'm in it with the whole común and I quarrel with someone, there are at least nine others to even the keel. With cooperatives, it's either all or none, in my opinion.
>
> —A vecino

The Valdemora farmer who is interested in increasing his wheat surplus, as all are, finds himself face-to-face with the issue of agrarian reform. There was no one who in 1963 did not recognize the need for mechanization to increase production. At that time, there were in use three types of mule-drawn plow—the Roman or crook plow with an iron share and two mold-board plows, one with a fixed and one with a rotating mold-board. The mold-board plows are not suited for as many varieties of terrain as is the Roman plow, but they both cut deeper. The deepest plow zone, about twenty centimeters, is produced by the fixed mold-board plow. Until the later 1950s, only the Roman plow was in use in the village. Valdemora was better mechanized in other respects: in 1963 there were two planters, three combines, and one reaper, all mule-drawn. None of these could be used on hillsides, however. There were also four generator-operated winnowing machines. Two or three vecinos of neighboring towns had tractors and more modern threshing-winnowing machines, and one or two Valdemora vecinos hired their services at threshing time. Otherwise, families threshed with the mule-drawn trillo and some winnowed by hand. Three small-scale and one large-scale farmer had no machinery at all and harvested with the scythe.

Everyone recognizes that the traditional land tenure system makes large-scale mechanization impossible, and all know that mechanized agriculture is more productive. Thus, the vecinos face the issue of modifying the system of land tenure—of yielding up their plots as they know them and as their grandfathers knew them. Villagers know that reorganization of the land base is not the only impediment to prosperous farming, for they know that a municipality of 267 hectares[1] should not be supporting ten or eleven farmers who want to be modern. It is well understood that the ultimate solution lies in the pattern of emigration and land rental. Already by 1963, one nearby Sierra village, a small aldea, had been abandoned by all of its vecinos. As they emigrated, they left the entire municipality in rent to a single man, who proceeded to farm it as a unit. Valdemorans feel that this will one day happen to their village, for they do not want their own sons to be farmers; but there is still a generation of vecinos who are committed to living in Valdemora. They find themselves in the position of having to do—sometimes almost wanting to do—things which Valdemora farmers have never done before.

There are two alternatives in the reorganization of farming, and each constitutes a major break with tradition. The first is the concentration of the land parcels to form larger plots. The farmers recognize that they cannot hope to accomplish this themselves. There have been repeated, isolated attempts at limited parcel concentration. For example, one Valdemora vecino wanted to make a single large plot where two of his strips lay on either side of a small strip belonging to another vecino. He offered to exchange a strip of equal size and quality for the one which separated his two plots. The second vecino refused: he said that the other man

1. This figure is a generous estimate of the total amount of cultivable land in Valdemora. Based on the 1935 figures, it is the total area of the municipality less the ducal lands, the railroad, roads, rivers, sheepwalks, and all structures. It includes the poor, unexploited lands lying between cultivable areas and the post-1935 railroad expropriations, so that the total is in reality somewhat lower.

would increase the productivity on that strip by the proposed concentration and that he ought to give more for the plot than one of precisely equal size. The first vecino did not consider this demand just and negotiation ceased. Such failures would only be multiplied in an attempt at village-wide reparcelation were the vecinos themselves responsible for its achievement. Each jealously guards what is his own, not wishing to contribute to another's prosperity and always assuming that others will be trying to put him at a disadvantage. The Spanish government has a parcel concentration service which sends specialists to study village cadasters and remap holdings and to give each vecino as much of each land type as he had previously, but in larger sectors. The service is available upon application. Valdemorans cannot reorganize their coveted land base through the council and expect to live together afterward as if nothing had happened. It is in such circumstances that they turn gratefully to the very outside forces they often resent. The government, because it does not have to live in Valdemora, will be able to effect blanket reparcelation. The council had made application for the service by 1963, but in 1967 Valdemora was still awaiting its turn.

Even with parcel concentration, mechanization makes greater sense when still wider tracts of land are cultivated as single units. This would require various owners to work their lands collectively, without respect for field boundaries. This constitutes an even greater break with tradition, requiring the vecinos to cooperate across household lines in those very activities where they have always most avoided cooperation. To join in this way would, of course, make parcel concentration unnecessary, but 1963 found the vecinos in a losing struggle against their traditional distaste for such a plan. It would have been possible to form a farming cooperative with or without government aid. As an officially registered village cooperative of the kind they were considering, for which a minimum of fifty hectares of wheatland (excluding fallow) must be united, the participants receive enough cash credit on machinery to cover the initial costs of mechanization: in 1963 this was 1200 pesetas per fanega of land in the first year, 600 pesetas per fanega in the second year, and 300 pesetas per fanega in the third year. In 1963, a cooperative with fifty hectares would have been able to purchase a tractor in its first year.

But there were serious drawbacks to accepting the government plan. In 1963, Valdemorans were only cultivating about fifty-five hectares of wheat in the municipality each year. Thus, unanimity was imperative in the formation of a village cooperative. The council was paralyzed by the lack of unanimity every time it met: no votes were taken, but nobody wished to call for one, for people sensed enough objections that they avoided formalizing their intransigence. This way, each vecino could say that "the others didn't seem to want to" without being able to say specifically "so-and-so voted no." The failure to unite embarrassed people, and everyone seemed to feel that his own negative feelings were partly to blame, for everyone had them. Then, there was the complaint that the government plan would have required the purchase of a Spanish tractor, when everybody wanted an English or American one. "And besides," everyone said, "we can always form a cooperative without the government." The tremendous disadvantage to an independent cooperative was that, without government aid, the participant vecinos would have had to put up the two hundred thousand pesetas for the new tractor which they wanted. Not everyone had such resources, so there the matter rested.

In mid-1963 the two vecino brothers who farm together bought a new (American) tractor. As joint farmers, they alone could unite enough land to make the purchase worthwhile. At least one other vecino knew of their plan to purchase and asked to join them. The brothers, sharing the view quoted at the head of this chapter, decided against extending their enterprise outside the family boundaries. They worked for themselves and, as a favor, began to cart grain from the fields for the one large-scale farmer who had no machinery at all and whose wife was ill. But they steadfastly refused to rent out the services of their tractor for pay, insisting that they had not bought it to make a profit from others.

More than a year after the first tractor came to Valdemora, one of the vecinos saw a second-hand tractor at a fair for a good price. He informed the vecino who had asked to join the brothers, and together they consulted two others about buying it as a group. Eventually, the four made the purchase without issuing invitations for more members. This event left four vecinos without access to a tractor: the balky, disliked head of Household 1, who had mule-drawn machinery; two vecinos with small holdings who had no machinery (the third had emigrated); and the man with a large holding who had no machinery either. The latter, whose two kinsmen were in the new group, was particularly hurt.

This was not the first time that neighbors had collaborated on the purchase of equipment which would have been too costly for them to purchase individually. The first piece of mule-drawn machinery in town, a binder, was put into use in 1928 by two vecinos in cooperation. In 1963, two different pairs of vecinos, in addition to the brothers, shared in the use of combines. One of these pairs (non-kin) remained intact with the purchase of the tractor; of the other pair (also non-kin), only one was in the new group. Finally, before the 1965 harvest, the whole común purchased a thresher.

With two tractors in town, the issue of cooperative farming assumed greater interest for more of the vecinos. In the winter of 1965–66, the alcalde was asked by provincial representatives of the agrarian extension program how Valdemora felt about cooperative plans, and the question was once again brought before the council, with favorable response. The vecino brothers with the new tractor proposed the formation of an official cooperative and offered to sell their machinery to the común—a tractor, a reaper, and a trailer, all recently purchased new. They had paid about 240,000 pesetas for these, and offered to sell them at 210,000 pesetas, allowing for depreciation. There was some discussion and the brothers lowered their price to 200,000 pesetas, upon which the común agreed. The success of this offer animated the vecino of Household 1 to offer the común his machinery. He had a half share in a mule-drawn combine, a winnower (outdated by the común's thresher), a mule-drawn planter, and a trailer. Of these, only the trailer was relatively new; the rest was older-vintage machinery of the type which several others also had but which would not serve a new mechanized operation. The común refused to purchase and he took offense, announced that he was no longer interested in discussing any cooperation, and left the meeting. The remaining vecinos decided to proceed without him. The six farmers with tractors had by now been able to expand their operations significantly and were by 1966 renting considerable land from families in neighboring villages who had emigrated en masse. Valdemorans no longer depended upon unanimity to unite the requisite number of hectares to form a cooperative.

At their next meeting, the four vecinos who owned the second tractor proposed to sell it to the común. The tractor had been purchased at least third-hand for 115,000 pesetas. They added to the offer various other pieces of machinery they had, also used, and asked of the común a total of 190,000 pesetas, allowing about 30 percent for depreciation. There was objection to that price for such old machinery, and the four finally lowered their price to 175,000 pesetas and requested some compensation for the cost of repairs which they had made after the purchase. The rest of the vecinos asked that the council meet again the next day and that the four bring in the receipts for the repairs so that a final price might be agreed upon. Somehow, the four never brought in the receipts, no agreement was reached, and the council again was unable to act. Next, a proposal developed to form two groups, one around the brothers' tractor and the other consisting of the group of four. The agrarian extension representatives inquired on the progress of the meetings and gave the alcalde the requisite forms to be filled out for the formation of cooperatives. The council met again and agreed to form the two groups (without Household 1); the vecinos carried home the forms to be signed, agreeing to meet again to turn them in in a few days' time.

When the appointed day came, no one had signed his form. People insisted that many issues must be resolved before they made their decision. For instance, one vecino raised the question of the shepherd: who would be responsible for the sheep while they were all farming together? Someone said it seemed logical to take weekly turns, but the man who had raised the question (who has no sheep) insisted that it must be the same person all the time. With this issue still unresolved, another vecino began to complain that he had never bought any machinery in his life and all of a sudden he was expected to put out an enormous sum for machinery—it seemed to him too much. At the same time, people had been advising the two brothers that they were bound to lose most by the grouping. They were indeed unhappy about the formation of two groups rather than one, although they continued to offer to form the core of the second group. But they also felt that they would end up doing all of the group's work since they were the only ones who knew how to drive the tractor. (They had not driven, either, until recently, but seemed to forget the ease with which they had learned.) With these objections, the negotiations broke down entirely. The alcalde became very angry that he had been made to lead on the government representatives and would now be embarrassed before them, when no one had wanted a cooperative from the beginning and had not been willing to say so.

Aside from all of the objections mentioned above, the vecinos knew that the formation of a cooperative would have forced them to deal with the problem of inequalities in land holdings. In villages where more depopulation had occurred, holdings were equalized by the rental and cultivation of emigrant families' lands which had lain fallow, for the remaining vecinos had not been able to cultivate all of them with the traditional techniques. In Valdemora, with the entire municipality under cultivation, the only apparent solution was for all vecinos to sell their lands to the común so that the harvest might be divided equally among them, but there was deep sentimental opposition to such a plan. At that time it was not possible to equalize holdings by cultivating the requisite amount in neighboring villages, for emigration had not yet proceded far enough, nor did Valdemorans possess enough machinery for such an operation. Also, this would have required the small holders to take on large amounts in rent, and this raised the same objections that pertained to the purchase of machinery. The council did not meet again on the question of cooperatives. The vecinos had proved unable to bring farming into the realm of común business. They opted instead for associational autonomy in farming and failed to activate the horizontal principles on which the común functions for other purposes.

The breakdown of the cooperative plan is hardly surprising in view of the sharp break with tradition which it requires. In one of Valdemora's smaller neighbors, where the government has already effected parcel concentration, the vecinos were also unable to cooperate to make the greatest use of mechanized techniques. There, six vecinos in rapid succession purchased their own tractors immediately after the fields were remapped. No one would cooperate with anyone else: now the bustling to and fro is with tractors rather than mule teams, but the inefficiency of the operation is in everyone's view the same as before. Further, no farmer has enough land to keep his tractor busy, and the machines are dormant much of the time. Valdemorans consider the purchase of six tractors in such a village ridiculous. In their own village, quite a different thing is beginning to happen.

By 1967, there were new cooperative plans to choose from, and the four vecinos who owned a tractor together had been able to rent enough land in neighboring villages to make participation possible. They purchased a second tractor and registered officially as an association under a plan which required a minimum of 150 hectares (including fallow) in wheat, barley, and oats.[2] They prefer to receive their government benefits in the form of chemical

2. The availability of such a plan paralleled the government move to create an official market for fodder grains. The increased demand for fodder in Spain arises from an increase in large-scale stock breeding in many areas. At the same time, with increased meat consumption, the consumption of bread—and thus the demand for wheat—have slumped.

fertilizers rather than machinery, and they work across field boundaries wherever two or more of them have adjacent holdings.

Gradually since 1963, the process of depopulation in neighboring towns has created an increasing supply of cultivable land there. The six Valdemora farmers who have three tractors between them have rented more and more grain land in other municipalities. The travel involved in working these rented lands was impossible without tractors, nor had the traditional techniques given the farmers time for such expansion. The full estate within the municipality was once the maximal unit which a farmer could work with his family's help;[3] today these limits have been broken, nor need a farmer's wife any longer go out to the fields to help him. The six men are working over eighty hectares of land outside the municipality alone, and still the brothers, who work proportionally the largest amount, say that they have only enough flat land to keep their tractor busy half the time.

Gradually and warily since the first tractor was brought to Valdemora, the vecinos are indeed extending the común's principles of mutual aid into farming activities. The official group of four is one example. The small cooperative has been quite successful and not beset by the expected jealousies: vecinos who are not members say that the four participants are well matched in terms of the sizes of their estates and the proportion of different land types within them. It was perhaps their tested ability to work together that made them wary of joining a village-wide cooperative. At the same time, the three farmers who might have formed a cooperative with the brothers are indeed not working in isolation. The brothers are renting the services of the tractor to each of them for harvesting. They cart the grain in to the threshing floors free

3. This was also near the minimum required for subsistence, replanting, and a security margin in case of famine. The subsistence level was approached more nearly before mule-drawn machinery came into use and is still evidenced on the few estates worked by mule-drawn plows and harvested by hand. Under the feudal regime, what today is marketable surplus from those estates was levied in taxes.

of charge for all three. Further, ever since they purchased the tractor, they had threshed free of charge for the vecino whose wife was unable to help him and who otherwise would have had to thresh his entire harvest alone with the mule-drawn tribulum. The común's purchase of a thresher suspended the latter arrangement. Until that time, threshing by tractor simply meant motorizing the tribulum, and winnowing remained a separate process, done by five vecinos with separate machines and by the rest by hand. The only vecino without access to a tractor, by his own choice, is the head of Household 1. He has on occasion hired tractor services for limited jobs, but usually deals with outside farmers rather than neighbors. His wife is the only woman who by 1966 was still going out to the fields at harvest time.

The new thresher rendered both the tribulum and the winnowing machine obsolete. It is interesting that the purchase and administration of the thresher were assumed by the común without difficulty, because mechanization does not require communalization of the threshing operation. The dried grain is brought to the individual threshing floors, as always, and the machine is taken from one to the other by adra. The machine is run by the tractor motors, the four members of the cooperative using their own, the group surrounding the brothers using theirs, and Household 1 tending to be served alternately by the two groups. Outside of the cooperative of four, the work force at any given threshing floor is formed by as many people as the job requires on the basis of their own convenience. The vecino of Household 1 is the only man who does not attend any threshing but his own. Thus, where communal control constitutes a threat to the areas in which the vecinos most treasure their independence, they have refused to turn affairs over to the común. Where their autonomy is less threatened, they still look to the común to regulate their affairs. Although vecinos criticize their own selfishness and point out that some pueblos have been successful in forming village-wide cooperatives, they feel that they have done what they think most necessary to preserve harmony in a generation of neighbors who intend not to emigrate, but to continue as farmers. It is perhaps significant that none of the smaller and more cohesive villages in the immediate area has been able to unite all of its vecinos in a single cooperative: it is in precisely those villages where formal disputes are unknown that the households have chosen to preserve the autonomy on which they feel the continued existence of the común depends.

While the común dealt with problems of agrarian organization, new developments turned the vecinos' attention to pastoral questions as well. In 1964, the Duchy more than doubled the price of rental of common lands (from 2250.00 pesetas to 5272.20 pesetas). There was a similar increase for other Sierra villages which had not already purchased their lands. Valdemorans decided to protest the increase. Vecinos from several villages were together in Medinaceli on another errand of local business and took the opportunity to talk with the ducal administrator, the owner of a small store who communicates orders from the active administrators of the estate. While the group was with the Medinaceli administrator and the Valdemorans were about to inquire the reason for the increase in rent, the vecinos from one of the other villages simply paid the rent due. The Valdemorans felt that protest was useless unless the villages stood together and, seeing their neighbors pay without question, they felt powerless to do anything but follow suit. (In fact, no organized protest had been arranged on the part of the various villages, so the turn of events was hardly surprising.) This was but a taste of things to come. During the following year, several Sierra villages received official notice from the Duchy that their common lands were being put on sale. In June 1966, Valdemora received its notice, giving six months' warning that the Duchy would put the lands on the market on 1 January 1967. The común thus faced the question of taking its option to buy back its lands.

The council postponed meeting formally on the problem of

ducal lands until more definitive word should come from the House of Medinaceli. A year passed. On San Antonio, in June, the vecinos settled their accounts as usual and intended to turn their rent over to the Duchy at year's end as if nothing had happened. If this were not accepted, they planned to establish a special bank account for the deposit of the rents, so that nobody might confiscate the lands on grounds of failure to pay rent. The woodlots for 1967 had already been staked out and each household had collected its fuel; the vecinos intended to do the same in 1968, but had no idea if the ducal forester would appear to mark off the area to be cut. While they were trying to proceed as normal, they were plagued by a number of questions.

Several issues center on the nature of the ducal rights in the village. The vecinos are uncertain of the exact number of hectares that the Duchy owns. They insist that the number stated in the modern cadaster is too high, for they know that the común in 1935 allowed many permanently fallow fields of low quality (*fincas perdidas*, lost or waste fields) to be surveyed as pasture, so that the Duchy rather than the vecinos would have to pay the land taxes on them. Having gained a real but temporary advantage, the vecinos now feel that the Duchy is trying to sell back lands that it does not rightfully own. They are unwilling to pay one thousand pesetas per hectare for their own fincas perdidas,[4] though those have been exploited as pasture through all the years of their disuse, and the Duchy has indeed had to pay the taxes on them. The vecinos have thus acquired an avid interest in knowing the exact amount of land to which the Duchy acquired rights in 1539. The difficulty here is that the documents concerning ducal rights do not include area measurements at all—the common meadow is referred to by its name and not its size, and the woodlands and pastures are simply designated as "those which are found within the municipality, bounded by such-and-such other municipalities

4. This is the price asked by the Duchy for common lands in the Sierra. The price applies equally to all common pasture, including meadow, and to woodland.

within the same valley." Valdemora's boundaries with its neighbors in adjoining valleys are even more imprecise and do not receive mention in the early documents, partly because each village used its own side of the hills for pasture and the more rugged tops of the hills were not used at all. Thus, for example, no specific boundary marker between Valdemora and Mazarulleque receives mention until 1801,[5] though the hill itself which lies between the two pueblos has long been known on both sides as el Mojonero, or the boundary-marker hill.

Also at issue is whether the Duchy acquired rights to the *suelo*, the land itself, or only to the *vuelo*, the produce of the land. Although the terms of the Duchy's agreements with the villages seem to refer only to vuelo—to leaves, grass, and woods—the nature of the Medinaceli tenure must also be studied with reference to the original royal grant to the Duchy. In no way are questions of feudal claims easily resolved, from either the village or the ducal point of view. In the Sierra Ministra, however, no village has yet contested feudal claims in a court, so that the issues of legality are moot questions. Rather, after a great deal of internal discussion, villages have invariably dealt with the Duchy on its own terms, accepting both the amounts of land on sale and the prices asked. Thus, while Valdemorans are taking such questions very much to heart, they are at the same time engaged in a very realistic discussion of what to do about their common lands when they are finally forced to either buy or release them.

Even fifty years ago, there would have been little question that the común must buy back its woods and pasture, for the meat and the fuel which they supported were indispensable to any household. Today, this is not the case. Particularly in the question of fuel, all families stand prepared to purchase butane stoves immediately if they are prevented from cutting wood. The issue surrounding the use of the pastures is more complex. No family still depends on its own flock for its meat supply, but the large stock

5. See Appendix, sec. 3, Miscellaneous: 1911.

owners owe most of their annual profit to the fact that they keep sheep. At 1963 prices, a flock of about 250 head brought in about forty-three thousand pesetas a year from the sale of lambs and wool. Families with sheep generally have as large a wheat surplus as other families, and it is income from the stock that has given them a far larger net annual profit than their neighbors without stock can hope for. But families without sheep are hardly willing to contribute equally to the purchase of the pastures from the Duchy, and Valdemora's commonlands contain no particularly large or profitable tracts of rich meadow or high quality woodland. Thus, with the notice of sale, the común, whose primary concern once was the maintenance of the balance between farming and herding interests, can no longer muster a unanimous decision for the purchase of the pastures. The acquisition of meat has become a family's private affair, independent of the común and of local conditions of pasturage. To farm and herd at the same time is now a question of choice rather than necessity.[6] The choice is being made—has long been in the making—in the direction of farming and away from herding. Some of the attitudes underlying this choice will be considered in the next chapter.

The problems besetting the común on the issue of pastures cannot be divorced from the interests of the individual vecinos as farmers. The case of the nonherders is obvious: it is simply pointless for them to pay as much as forty thousand pesetas each to preserve the pastures. The herders—and essentially only the three with large flocks in 1967—are faced with the possibility of having

6. This is borne out by the history of the sale of ducal lands in other villages. The common lands of the Sierra villages have long been on the market, though the issue of repurchase was apparently not pressed until now. Several larger towns near Valdemora purchased their lands from the Duchy as long as fifty or sixty years ago. In these cases, the común invariably made the purchase as a unit, all vecinos contributing equally to the cost. In villages where the sale has been more recent, the divergence of herding and farming interests is evident—independent groups of vecinos have in several cases made the purchase when the común members could not reach a unanimous decision to purchase as a group.

to buy the pastures themselves. The cost to each would be equivalent to at least half of the price of a tractor. They are doubting the value of such an investment. Now, as never before, it would be possible for them instead to put both their money and their manpower into expanding their farm operations—into more machinery and the rental and cultivation of more of the fields left by emigrants in neighboring villages. The moment has not yet come for the final decision, but some vecinos believe it entirely possible that soon there will be no more herding in Valdemora.

The different interests of herders and nonherders have even been brought to bear on that once-vital piece of land, the prado, or common meadow (also part of the ducal holding). This was once essential grazing land for draft animals, both cows and mules. Now, without cows and with the number of mules greatly reduced by the use of motorized machinery, the meadow is little used. Instead, since the tractors came to town, the común has grown hay on the prado and divided the harvest equally among all the households. But by 1966, farmers without sheep were in favor of turning such a fertile area over to wheat, while stock owners were interested in having their shares of the hay for their sheep in winter. Thus, the meadow as well as the sheep pasture had acquired different value in the eyes of vecinos with different interests. Stock owners themselves admitted that they could do without that amount of hay and that an equal share in the prado's wheat harvest would be worth more; the use of the meadow seemed destined to change again, but it is still the común which has the power of decision and administers the meadow's use.

On one issue concerning the ducal pastures there is no divergence of opinion. If none of the vecinos chooses to buy back the pastures, the común as a body will try to prevent its use as grazing land by an outsider, for people are afraid that this will force them, as farmers, to open their stubble and fallow to the owner of the pastures. Whether this can actually be required of them is perhaps another moot question, but if such a thing occurred, the farmers would be confined to cultivating only half of the municipality each year. Machinery, time, and chemical fertilizers are beginning to permit them to use more of the land each year, and if it is not for their own sheep, they are not interested in maintaining the present form of biennial rotation. In self-defense and in defense of its members' interests as farmers, the común is considering breaking the spatial continuity of the pastures by cultivating at random all over the municipality, if this is not judged illegal (that is, if pasture does not legally include the stubble-grazing rights in such situations.) This would render stubble and fallow land virtually useless as pastoral resources, leaving only the poorer areas above the cultivable fields.

The común's fight in this potential case would be against having to deal with outsiders on subjects which should by tradition constitute internal business only. With the gradual decline of pastoral interests, the común finds its interests best served by breaking the balance which it once functioned to maintain, though people do not expect to be pushed to such an extreme. As its individual members look increasingly toward only farming for their livelihood, the común is gradually—more slowly than the individuals who compose it—finding its own attention focused on how best to maintain the new balance, not between farming and herding, but between the independent and expanding operations of the farmers themselves. In the transitional period when mechanized farming is just beginning, much of the común's business seems to revolve around the liquidation of its own interests in the farming and herding economy which the vecinos themselves are finding outdated. But the reactivation of the adra for new purposes, the mobilization for self-defense against outsiders, and the very fact that vecinos are concerned for their internal harmony give evidence that the común, as a focus of sentiment and as a problem-solving organization, is simply assuming a new face for the present generation of vecinos. The council's agenda is changing radically, although the assumptions upon which the común's existence rests are the same.

Lest these paragraphs be mistaken for the apologistic message that there is tradition in change, I hasten to emphasize that the común is assuming a new face *for the present generation* of adult farmers. A Valdemoran would say, "Yes; but remember, this is the *last* generation." The expectation—indeed the hope—is that in twenty-five years the population of Valdemora will consist of one or two "really modern" farmers, but not enough to form a común. The rate of emigration surely makes this a reasonable expectation, and today's vecinos actually look upon emigration as the only peaceable and thus the only desirable means by which farming in Valdemora can become fully modernized. And lest the vecinos be misconstrued as prophets of doom, I should repeat that, far from pessimism, they view their children's emigration and the depopulation of the farm community as desirable ends. They do not know if the one or two "really modern"farmers of the future will be sons of the pueblo or if today's younger farmers will emigrate, to be replaced by men who have had formal studies in agronomy. Some feel that the very houses of today, and the sites on which they stand, will be unused for habitation. They cite the initiation of a movement to consolidate village councils (parallel to the consolidation of ayuntamientos) which may unite the farmers of twenty or more one-time villages in single comunes de vecinos in the traditional centers of the region. "These houses," predicts one vecino, "if they are used at all, will be used for storage. Farmers will have new houses, in places like Sigüenza where there are central medical facilities and things like that. They'll drive their cars to their fields and drive home at night; they'll live like *señores*." The movement of farmers toward local centers has already begun in some parts of the Sierra provinces.

The creation of consolidated comunes de vecinos is but a step beyond the formation of cooperatives as it is now occurring in the villages. But, like the cooperatives, a new común can bear only limited resemblance to the traditional one I have described here. Like the cooperatives which precede them, they will be special-purpose groupings whose economic focus far outshadows questions of sentiment and whose members are united by legal rather than extra-legal bonds. No longer will the común encompass the entire community or offer a way of life.

# 7 Change II: The Style of Life

Nobody wants to be a shepherd. The shepherd isn't a complete man.

—A vecino

If I could have anything I wished for, I would wish for a flat in Madrid. Not to stop working—to go on working but to change locale.

—A vecino

As Valdemorans review the documents concerning their village, they see as the key to the changes which have taken place the dislike for herding and the opposed tendency to exploit land agriculturally as much as possible while still providing the table with meat. Villagers are unanimous on this issue. They are also unanimous in viewing their history as one of their own making—a series of rational choices from among possible alternatives—and thus they interpret their history as the story of the gradual emergence of a preferred style of life. That they have been able to make active choices they owe to factors in the world outside, from which they recognize no separation—factors such as the varying availability of land, new techniques, or the market demand for various products. The vecinos' consciousness of their relatedness within a larger universe is marked. "We've expanded farm operations thanks to emigration from the other towns," says one vecino, "but there's a limit to that, too, and pretty soon we're going to find out that we're still crowded." Another says, "We're starting to plant less wheat and more fodder grains, because the increase in stock breeding in other parts of the country is going to bring a good market for fodder."

When the vecinos reviewed the cadaster of 1750, all commented

TABLE 8

Livestock Other Than Sheep

| Year | Cows and Oxen[a] | Mules[b] | Asses[c] | Horses[d] | Goats[e] | Pigs[f] |
|---|---|---|---|---|---|---|
| 1750 | 54 | 5 | 20 | 16 | 0 | 20 |
| 1879 | 28 | 16 | 0 | 10 | 7 | ? |
| 1963 | 2 | 19 | 0 | 5 | 2 | 25 |

[a] For draft and/or milk
[b] For draft
[c] For breeding
[d] For breeding and transport
[e] For milk
[f] For meat

on the amount of land then dedicated to meadow and on the number of cows and oxen kept (see table 8), but they interpreted the difference from the present situation as the simple result of the gravitation toward the attractions of marketing wheat, given improving techniques, which has led vecinos to cultivate meadowland as they simultaneously replace draft cattle with mules.[1] They have chosen modernization in the agricultural sphere, and they speak consciously of using the advances in farming as levers against the demands of herding. Gradually, even the importance of supplying the village tables with meat from the village's own herds has begun to disappear. Although we might argue that the modern villager is unable to know the motives of his ancestors, we must concede that the motives imputed explain the data of the past as fully as they typify the present: nobody wants to be a shepherd.

The Cadaster of the Marqués de la Ensenada lists, in 1750, the presence in Valdemora of eight hired hands. Of these, two are specifically named shepherds, and four field hands (and the remaining two were probably field hands as well). When every family kept sheep (see table 9) as well as larger stock, and before

1. Meadowland amounted to 35.50 hectares in 1750, 24.66 hectares in 1879, and 3.65 hectares in 1963.

TABLE 9

Sheep Ownership

| Year | Number of Vecinos | Number of Sheep Owners | Average Herd Size | Range of Herd Sizes | Total Number of Sheep |
|---|---|---|---|---|---|
| 1750 | 9 | 8 | 104 | 28–178 | 832 |
| 1877 | 14 | 13 | 83 | 20–416 | 1085 |
| 1963 | 11[a] | 6[b] | 151 | 56–246 | 907 |

[a] Includes the non-vecino of Household 12.

[b] By 1966, this number was reduced to 5, because one vecino with a flock of about 200 head ceased to herd.

any agricultural operations were mechanized, considerable labor was required for farming, and one person had to devote his full time to herding. Families expanded their labor supply by hiring year-round help. Further, they hired temporary help at the harvest season, contracting itinerant harvesters on the fair days dedicated to this end (Santa Librada, 20 July, and Santiago, 25 July). The most frequent hiring was of adult labor, and households fell back on their own younger or older people for herding. None of the hired hands on record was a native of the village.

Today there are no hired hands living in Valdemora. In 1963, one or two families still hired temporary labor for the harvest, but by 1966 this practice also had become obsolete. The use of farm machinery had made it possible to perform the same operations, and more, with a smaller labor force, freeing even some of the family from extensive participation in the harvest. At the same time, whether or not a family keeps sheep is determined largely by the amount of labor available within the family without recourse to outside hiring. The absence in town of hired shepherds is much older than the absence of field hands and is probably more than a century old. Professional shepherds, who have always been outsiders, still hire out, but no family is willing to pay their price, which in 1963 was twenty-four thousand pesetas a year in addition to room and board. The small scale of sheep herding in the area does not repay such an expense. Thus, many contemporary vecinos have kept sheep when their grown sons assumed farming duties, but when the sons married and the households separated, neither fathers nor sons maintained flocks any longer. The professional shepherd commands a high price because few are willing to do his job. Families cease keeping sheep for the same reason, now that they do not depend on that for meat: they do not want their sons to be shepherds. The distaste for herding is greater than that for farming and of a different order. The demands of herding run counter to some of Valdemorans' deepest feelings about what life should be like.

In terms of physical exertion, the shepherd's work is lighter than the farmer's, evidenced by the fact that both children and old people herd more often than they farm. The hours required are long, but the pace is easy for anyone who is not severely disabled physically. The only season of discomfort is the winter, but then the hours of grazing are relatively short and confined to days when there is no precipitation. On many winter days, when the weather is bad or when the ground is covered with snow, the sheep are stall-fed. Rather than from exertion, the shepherd suffers from isolation. The evil of his physical isolation is that it engenders social isolation as well, and this is a heavy burden in Valdemoran terms.

The shepherd, unlike the farmer, does not work with or near other people. His duty is to stay away both from the fields and from other flocks. Whereas the farmer generally comes home to lunch, the shepherd does not, and thus he misses the main family gathering of the day. In summer, when the sheep graze at night, the herder sleeps while the town is awake and works while the town is asleep. The needs of the animals keep him busy on days when other people are celebrating fiestas, attending mass, and visiting together. The shepherd's participation in the pueblo social life is determined by the season and the weather, but is in any case limited. He is the only villager who does not pass the fountain and the lavadero with frequency or at their busiest hours. His chief contacts are in his own family kitchen, and his other contacts are often second-hand. In the terms which define the basis of community life, the shepherd is a marginal person. The less contact he has with others, the less control others have over him. When the shepherd is of a común family, the loss of control is not too serious. When the shepherd is an outsider, the fact that he cannot pass before the communal jury and does not have a known family background to answer for him makes him susceptible to the worst expectations or suspicions. It is his life as this kind of outsider which makes the professional shepherd a social outcast in a region where social control and physical nucleation are both very tight.

The case of the professional throws light on the less extreme case of the man who herds in his own town. Men who work as full-time herders in their own communities are not regarded as professional shepherds for the following reasons: they live amongst their own kinsmen and fellow villagers; they do not wander from village to village in the normal course of their work; they do not contract as herders in any but their own families, though they may then take on small numbers of animals from one or two other families; they are members of farm families with inherited shares in village estates; they know how to farm and can at any time exchange roles with other men of the family, which happens with some frequency; and, finally, their herding is conceived as part of the family enterprise, and they are not people who would for any reason herd outside of that enterprise or emigrate as herders. In contrast, the professional shepherd is an outsider by definition. Notions about shepherds which are weak or dormant with respect to native herders are intensified with respect to professionals.

The more itinerant the outsider is, the greater is the contempt in which he is held. Thus, next to Gypsies, the most despised groups are migrant herders and itinerant tradesmen or farm hands, for they are assumed to live outside the context of sedentary—and thus "civilized"—society.[2] In the Sierra Ministra there is only sporadic contact with such peoples, but the attitudes toward all of them are similar. The nearest groups of rural but nonfarming people are the long-distance transhumant shepherds of merino stock, descendants of the herders of the Royal Mesta. Valdemora still lies on their transhumance route, now by railroad freight lines, and merino herders from central Castile pass through the town twice a year. The villagers' view of them exemplifies the general attitude toward rural nonfarmers and migrants: they are viewed with amusement, with condescension, and with some degree of apprehension. They are considered picturesque, but clumsy in style, backward, and ill-bred; the apprehension with which they are viewed has partly to do with questions of sexuality.

The person who is continually isolated from the intensive contacts which others enjoy is forced into a kind of celibacy which Valdemorans view as dangerous for normal development. Even the native shepherd has less chance than his farmer-brother to enter noviazgo—partly because of his eternal absence from the scene and partly because his occupation makes him an undesirable mate. Valdemorans do not blind their eyes to the realities of human sexual needs. The professional shepherd in this sense is like the priest. The priest's case shows that one need not be physically

2. Similar feelings are widespread in all the areas of Spain with which I am familiar. Along the north coast there are various groups of herding and/or peddling peoples who, although often regarded locally as separate races, are best viewed as "occupational outcasts" for reasons of commercial itinerancy and/or local or long-distance transhumancy. Examples are the cowherding Pasiegos of Santander, the cowherds of "Alzada" in Asturias, and the Maragatos of León. The latter group is largely itinerant and commercial. Although a group like the Pasiegos are locally-transhumant herders in their own territory, much of Pasiego emigration has taken place via certain forms of itinerant commerce. Galicia has also produced large numbers of professional herders, farm hands, and peddlers, selling their services and their wares in many parts of the country but remaining outsiders in the communities where they work.

removed from the scene of activities to be a social isolate, for he also is one. Priests (who are always outsiders) and full-time shepherds are seen as celibates of the same ilk, and celibacy is thought to be unnatural. These people, then, are prey to perversions, or at best to illicit liaisons, which afford them their only outlets for sexual satisfaction. The case of the shepherd is, of course, less clearcut than that of the priest, and many shepherds have ample opportunity to marry.[3] But the youngster who goes into herding is courting danger. In a culture where adult status is best achieved through marriage and the establishment of a household, where bachelor status forces people into mozo groups long after they have outgrown them, and where adulthood is practically coterminous with parenthood and family headship, unmarried people are necessarily marginal in many respects. The individual who actually chooses or knowingly exposes himself to the possibility of a celibate life is more of an outsider than ever, though he may play crucial roles in the economy and the social structure. The priest is at least repaid with some prestige, status, and power. The shepherd has none of these. Valdemorans are unwilling to see their sons as either priests or shepherds. The fact that to date no Valdemoran has entered the priesthood and that they are now shunning herding as well, because they can afford to, speaks for the strength of the sentiment against these forms of social isolation.

Normal bachelorhood contrasts with the celibate life of the priest or shepherd, for the bachelor's celibacy is an accident of his personal history which emerges even as he lives continually surrounded by others: it is not accompanied by monastic isolation, spiritual or physical. The differing attitudes toward the bachelor shepherd and the bachelor farmer, even when they are

3. My impression is that there is a higher rate of bachelorhood among shepherds in the region than among farmers, though the disappearance of full-time herders from the region makes demonstration difficult. An important distinction between farmer and shepherd bachelors is in their statuses in the social structure, to be discussed presently.

both natives of the común, bring into relief once again the importance of the physical nucleation of the community.

The Sierra Ministra knows no dispersion of settlement except where a few roadside establishments have recently been built along the main highway away from town centers. These are few, because the road is dotted with valley towns. In the villages, the town center and the surrounding countryside are sharply distinguished terminologically. Within the nucleus where humans reside, one is "in the pueblo," either "at home" *(en casa)* or "in the street" *(en la calle)*. Within this nucleus, all reference is to man-made landmarks—to the houses, barns, and hen-houses of the various vecinos, to the streets, the fountain, the lavadero, the store, the church. But a single step beyond the last house in any direction, one is suddenly "in the country" *(en el campo)*. Here, to be outdoors is much different from being "in the street" within the town center, though at points el campo begins much closer to the pueblo than is the church, which is not in the pueblo and still not in the "country." These usages serve, thus, to unite even the relatively distant church and station barrio with the pueblo and to set all of them apart from the natural landscape which surrounds them. Valdemorans pity those who live in the isolated commercial establishments on the road—"all alone in the country"—and regard these ventures as dubious ways to make a better living. A house is "in the country" even if it stands in sight of other houses. To be in a pueblo, it must be very near not only to other houses but also to a church, a fountain and lavadero, a store, and a plaza. A distance of five minutes' walk is already "far" in the Sierra, and at this distance separate barrios may be identifiable.

The farmer must leave the intensely social scene of habitation and human contacts to work daily in the countryside, where his mission is conceived as a struggle against the elements and against fate. But the coordinated rotation and the use of common roads, in addition to the frequent company of another household member, keep him in close contact with other farmers. He returns to the village, often even during the busy harvest, to take his midday meal and to water his mules, and again before nightfall. The night is something like the countryside itself: one does not want to be out in it. The shepherd, as I have said, is committed both to the countryside and to the night. This fact alone makes his life hard and sad and sets him apart from other men. In the recent past, the herder's displacement from the pueblo was even more pronounced. Before the crossing of municipal boundaries was prohibited, shepherds grazed their flocks over longer distances. This apparently sometimes involved sleeping in the pastures and brought the condition of the native shepherds of the past closer to that of the despised migrants of the present day.

The shepherd is forced, by definition, out of the ken of the community which depends upon physical presence for social control. The farmer, on the other hand, continues to live in the bosom of that community. The sexual morality of the bachelor farmer is not subject to the same implicit doubt as that of the bachelor herder who may be his brother. Because the farmer is in constant view of his neighbors, keeping the same schedule that they keep, his movements are known. More important, because he lives continually among others, even though celibate, he is not thought to suffer from lack of sexual satisfaction. Here emerges the notion that strong sexual needs grow out of a life of isolation and are not the necessary product of bachelorhood. The single person who lives among others is thought not to experience sexual desire to the same degree as the person who lives in isolation. Thus, the shepherd's sexuality is more exaggerated also than that of the priest and constitutes the greater threat—hence the peculiar apprehension with which herders and other migrants are regarded when they pass through town.

The bachelor farmer, anomalous as his household may be, achieves vecino status. A man, married or single, cannot achieve this status except as a farmer, working his inherited lands. The shepherd, married or single, unless he is also a farmer, is always but an adjunct to a household. Living apart from the locus of community control, he can be morally suspect, and he occupies a marginal and powerless position in the social structure.[4]

The depth of the bias against herding makes obvious why Valdemorans were willing to turn to outside sources for meat when it became possible to do so. The widow Josefa speaks of a past when "there were no butchers." No one is sorry that now there are butchers, though there is some nostalgia for the old, elaborate meriendas which accompanied fiestas and for the excitement of families' joint slaughter days. In retrospect, many events of the traditional year were tied to the need for redistributing meat, and these have begun to disappear rapidly. In the last years of the operation of the communal oven, when people were getting their meat from butchers, the position of hornero was no longer auctioned. It was handled instead by adra, and it no longer gave rise to a feast. Similarly, the común no longer even bothers to auction off manure. Likewise, the feast of San Antonio no longer performs a necessary function in redistributive terms, and it is the only surviving fiesta of its kind. In short, a previously redistributive community has responded to the alternative of marketing its sheep and buying its meat from professional butchers. In so doing, a family need not keep sheep or send its sons out to herd, and those who continue herding are responding to the demands of an outside market rather than to the needs of the community.

The attractions of producing for the market have been responsible for vast changes on the agricultural scene. First cattle and then mules have become obsolete with the continual adoption of new techniques. As cattle disappeared as draft animals, so also did the need for a cowherd. The cultivation of larger and larger

4. The cowherd, by contrast, was a vecino (or vecinos by turn) whose duties took him only to the town common, adjacent to the population center. A further idea of the shepherd's marginal position can be gained with reference to similarly structured communities in the northern peninsula—for example, Rio de Onor (Dias 1953)—where the care of the sheep and/or goats is always relegated to an outsider on contract, while larger stock are herded by the villagers themselves.

amounts of land in wheat, including meadows, has changed the village landscape, and the new forms of joint farming and parcel concentration are changing it even more. The farmer's ability to work more land now takes him across village lines, for his power-driven machinery has obliterated the old notion of distance. He travels voluntarily farther than the shepherd does, but he returns home at the same hour as before. He no longer needs hired hands, and the labor fairs of July no longer exist. The council is less concerned with maintaining an effective mixed economy than with aiding the cause of efficient farming.

With the disappearance of auctions and feasts, the council's functions lose much of the quality that once attracted folklorists. If some of the remaining events of the fiesta cycle are celebrated with less vigor than before, it is perhaps because these are no longer the only available forms of diversion. Improved communications and mass media make visiting and entertainment easier. The events which people say are observed less today than in the past are such affairs as the meriendas of Todos los Santos and Carnival Thursday. These perhaps suffer most from competition with new forms of entertainment. But the celebration of many impromptu meriendas within común subgroups on Sundays or other feast days indicates that this form of diversion has not lost its importance. Similarly, the major village fiestas are celebrated on perhaps a greater scale than before, for visitors travel with ease from all over central Spain.

Valdemorans are not attracted to efficient farming for its own sake but, rather, for what they can buy with the profit. The extremely high value which they place on education makes the further schooling of their children their most important goal. They do not think of "studies" just as a means to greater earning power, but value them for their own sake. This attitude should be emphasized, because it is not shared by all Spanish parents who are eager to train their children. In some regions, studies matter little if one "lives well"—be it as a landlord, a clever businessman, or a well-salaried employee. The Sierra provinces have a reputation for producing very hard workers and few illiterates.[5] I did not fully appreciate this characterization until I became familiar with parts of Castile where success is defined largely in monetary terms and where many villagers "don't do anything"—that is, they live from rents and are hard put to describe themselves in any other terms at all. Valdemorans place no value on a life of idleness, though a life of comfort is a desideratum. They tend not to classify people on the basis of the fortunes they wield, but rather on the hard work and integrity with which they achieved them. Retirement from work comes with old age, not with financial success alone. Finally, the learned professions requiring long studies are held in highest regard. The wealthy businessman earns greater esteem if he sends his children to university, for wealth is a means by which to achieve learning, and learning alone is valued for itself.

The value placed on learning per se and on the professions is interesting because it does not relate to goals which any Valdemoran expects to see achieved in his family in his lifetime. Vecinos' own children do well to complete their secondary education (that is, to receive the *bachillerato*) or some vocational training, or both, for even these involve considerable expense and removal from the pueblo. No vecino's child in memory has entered one of the esteemed professions; only in the ranks of long-established emigrants, in the hazier areas of the genealogies, is this a possibility. Most Valdemorans, when they emigrate, move into blue-collar and a few into office jobs. The important immediate end of urban emigration in the villager's terms is not the attainment of great comfort and success, which are rare, but the rearing of the emigrant's children in an atmosphere which will allow them to go farther than their parents could. This long-range vision greatly influences the style of emigration. People choose to move to major

5. In Valdemora in 1963 there was only one person who was not fully literate. This was one of the old women, who is able to write but cannot, for lack of practice, read print.

capitals in Spain. There is, as I have said, almost no participation in the enormous Spanish working-class migration into other European countries, for the locus and style of life in those situations are not favorable to the Valdemoran's aims. He would rather hold a lower-paying factory job in Barcelona than a more lucrative one in Paris, because the locus of his family life and his children's future should be in Spain. Further, of all possible vocations, no Valdemoran has yet chosen to study agronomy, for the goal is simply not to return to the village—to *any* village—as a farmer. Farming is considered healthful but hard work. It is not injurious to personal development as is herding, nor is it necessarily more insecure than is a salaried job, but nobody wants to raise his children in a pueblo when he can raise them instead in a city.

Keeping pace with the urban emigration has been the gradual evolution of a new life style in the pueblo itself. Examination of change in the areas where data are best—such as the sexual division of labor—shows the emergence of patterns which are bringing Valdemorans closer to their ideals and sheds light on the nature of those ideals.

The vecino's life has become easier because, first, he no longer has to keep sheep, do his own butchering, and so on. Second, his farming itself involves shorter hours, even on an expanded land base, and less physical labor, because it has been mechanized. For women, these same changes have brought freedom from participation in most agricultural tasks. The change in the woman's daily round in particular has given the pueblo an entirely new aspect.

As recently as 1963, in the months of heavy work surrounding the harvest, a visitor would find the town deserted throughout the day. Men were in the fields, and their sons with them. In spring, whole families went together to weed the fields of growing grain. Then, while the men plowed the ground for the fall planting, their wives and daughters took on the task of preparing and planting the vegetable gardens and the potato and chick-pea fields.

This was followed by the harvesting of vetch, barley, wheat, and oats, in that order, and the threshing and winnowing of all these crops. The worst of the harvest was over by mid-August, but most of the threshing and winnowing remained. In August, the chick-peas as well were harvested and threshed. September was a relatively light month for women, but men's autumn was occupied still with plowing and then with planting the next year's crop. The potatoes were harvested in October and beets in early November. Women were heavily occupied in the latter tasks while the cereal planting still occupied the men.

The grain harvest involved women as well as men and called the entire family away from other tasks. Many fields were harvested by hand. Even with mule-drawn reapers, there remained the gleaning and binding to do by hand. After the shocks were dried, they were gathered in and the long processes of sledge-threshing and winnowing followed. The days of the grain harvest were the only ones of the year when a family often did not eat the noon meal at home. With bread and meat for snacks, many stayed in the fields from daybreak to sundown. The women worked in heavy stockings to protect them against the stubble, long sleeves to protect them against the stickles of the grain itself, and heavy scarves to shield them from the scorching sun. In the village kitchens, the chick-pea cocido for whatever meal the family took at home was left to stew slowly and untended in the *hornacha,* a straw-burning wall-oven used primarily in this season. Only the very old and the very young were left in the pueblo; a young child was cared for by an older child or a grandparent if its mother was in the fields. The woman who had to stay at home with an infant left her husband to struggle under an enormous load.

A visitor to Valdemora during the 1966 harvest might have thought it a different town. Morning activities centered around the lavadero and the shop and vendors as at any other time of year. Every afternoon, the house doors stood open and groups of women and girls sat together sewing and embroidering. The men brought the tractors in at midday and had lunch at home. The hornachas were no longer in use. Men were doing what had previously been the work of the whole family on a daily schedule which permitted them to take on much of the gardening as well and still to spend some whole mornings or afternoons in the pueblo on other affairs. Only the shepherd's work did not change in this three-year period, but where the shepherd had previously lent a hand in the harvest during a few spare hours, he, too, now enjoyed free time.

I have written of shepherds in these chapters as if they were invariably men. This is true today, but a generation ago it was not. Under the pressures of the summer schedule which I have described, or in the winter lambing season, women often herded sheep and freed their husbands or sons for heavier tasks.[6] The advent of mule-drawn machinery on the agricultural scene in the early part of the century freed women from herding just as further mechanization has now freed them from agriculture as well. Any older village woman knows the routines of herding and the routes through the pastures, but it is forty years since she has had to use this knowledge. When she is asked about herding, she refers to it as "men's work" (as is farming) and does not associate herself with it. Similarly, documents always refer to shepherds as male. The complex of facts, past and present, leads us to conclude that there is an ideal sexual division of labor which affects terminological usage and, further, leads informants to minimize the areas in which the ideal could not or cannot be achieved. A woman will expect admiration for her gardening of flowers, but not of her vegetables, though she gardens both. When an old woman speaks of the work load she carried in the past, she cites cooking for large groups of harvesters, spinning wool, and making

6. There is no local evidence of women as full-time shepherds, but this would not be surprising. Women were voting members of the local *mestas* which were forerunners of the Royal Mesta.

items of clothing which today are purchased, but not herding or threshing.

A review of all the data at hand suggests that there are few kinds of work which are today thought of as "men's work" which have not at some time been done by women as well. In the limited time perspective offered by documents and life histories, there is no evidence of women either plowing or participating in construction projects, including cendera. Nor is there evidence for females as shearers, weavers, or manufacturers of tools and equipment. It is from the heaviest tasks and from the trades that women are generally absent. Conversely, men do many things that are considered women's work: if there is need, they perform household chores, shop, and cook for themselves, or tend children. Things which they do not do are launder and sew: one widower walks to the next village to leave his laundry and mending with a kinswoman but keeps house for himself in all other respects. Another thing men do not do is assist women in childbirth. But there is, in general, a large sphere of activities in which in practice the sexual division of labor is not rigid. By contrast, the ideal suggests much greater rigidity.

Two generations ago, the ideal separation of male and female spheres of activity would have been visible almost solely in ritual contexts—in the separate feasting of the two sexes, the separate ritual duties assigned to each, their separate positions in church and in processions—or in their different forms of leisure. Ritual and leisure, of course, stand a bit apart from the economic necessities of daily life. With the easing of the latter, the quality of daily living may be seen more and more to approximate the ideal which was once expressed only in ritual and leisure. Valdemorans in the pueblo today enjoy a work schedule and patterns of social life which closely resemble those of their relatives in the cities. Aside from the fact that the farmer does not have paid vacations, what young Valdemorans feel most lack of is the commercial establishments in which they might spend their leisure time—

movie houses, cafés, a variety of shops—and populated streets and parks through which to make the paseo.

The Valdemoran concern with the physical proximity of houses to one another and of individuals to the center of population density has emerged in a variety of contexts. I have suggested that the physical circumscription of the area in which social life is lived serves both to define the religious community and to perpetuate it. I believe we must regard this physical circumscription of the social scene as a cultural ideal which underlies many of the changes which have taken place. We might call this the "instinct to huddle." Because it brings people together in ways which are considered crucial, physical clustering is fundamental to the ideal style of life. As an ideal which people strive to achieve, it underlies the form which new settlements take, the decline of herding, and the magnetic attraction of urban centers.

Another fundamental ideal, but one which has not always been as visible as it is now, is the separation of male and female in public aspects of their lives. In some respects, this ideal includes the notion that certain activities are appropriate to only one of the sexes and not the other, at least in public. But equally important is the simple notion that, outside the confines of the home, associational patterns should separate the two sexes, even in the performance of the same activity. This notion underlies the traditions which unite people on the basis of their sex and separate them from the other sex even when they are observing an event in ways which are otherwise identical (for example, celebrating the same mass or sharing identical foods at a feast). This ideal is no less fundamental for the fact that it has not always been expressed on as many levels as at present. The wealthy have always been able to maintain and display it more easily than the poor, and Valdemorans are not wealthy.

Separation of the sexes is more generally important than that of age groups, though the latter is quite marked in Valdemora's corporate tradition. It is interesting that in Spanish villages which have only enough pupils to occupy two schoolteachers, boys and girls are taught separately, although curricula are identical. Thus, each teacher is faced with pupils of all ages. Age-graded schools are only instituted in large populations. Valdemorans realize that age-graded classes offer their children better training than the one-room village school, and this constitutes part of the attraction of urban emigration.

Separation of settlement from the countryside, separation of male and female in public social life, and formal education of children can be viewed as goals which are imperfectly achieved in village life. The possibility of achieving them more perfectly in nonrural occupations and urban settings makes the villager at base a socially mobile person.

A Valdemoran is able to behave correctly in a much wider variety of social contexts than are visible within the limits of the village, for these are parts of his universe. He knows whom to address by the title *Don* although in the village he addresses only the priest in this way. He knows to whom to say *su servidor* (your servant), though he never uses the expression in the limits of his village. He knows to remove his *boina* (beret) in the city, although he wears it even in his own kitchen when he is in the village. (In Valdemora, the wearing of the boina generally signifies age and occupation: a mozo will assume it when he takes on a major role in farming; a mozo who does not farm does not wear it unless he performs manual labor. In this region, the boina sets apart the rural, manual laborer from men of other rural occupations and from young boys.) He employs a dual set of table manners—one for his own kitchen and pueblo fiestas, even though invited outsiders may be present, and one for use outside the confines of the home or común, in the bar or in public contexts outside the village. The almost exclusive use of the knife in eating, the eating of certain foods from communal plates, use of the communal *porrón* or wine jug, disappear in the latter contexts. In the city kitchen, these are rusticisms which distinguish recently emigrated families from longer established ones. Certain linguistic habits change and some words (such as *adra*) disappear from the vocabulary and are unknown to emigrants' children. These are, of course, only a few of the outer characteristics of the farmer—he cannot so easily change the way he walks or the fact that he looks somewhat uncomfortable wearing a necktie. But the point I wish to emphasize is that, even as a villager, he has learned behavior appropriate to contexts outside village life and he teaches these to his children. So, to some extent, does the schoolteacher, but not in all of the respects I have mentioned.

No detailed survey of común affairs or of the leveling force of gossip at the lavadero can demonstrate the degree to which the Valdemoran is part of the class system or the way he regards that system and is prepared to play roles, interpret signals, and fulfill ambitions within it. Whatever ambitions and experience the villager has in the larger system are due to his contacts outside the común in the amorphous networks discussed in chapter 5. It is through these networks, and not through membership in the común that children of different families are exposed to different parts of the outside world and in different ways. It is within their own households that behavioral examples are impressed upon them and different kinds of ambition encouraged. The schoolteacher at best conveys the rudiments of etiquette. A campaign to serve the children lunch in the school "so that they'll learn to eat better" had brief success in 1966 but was abandoned after the cook, one of the mozas, married. The necessary preparations seemed too elaborate for a village where children were all five minutes' walk from home. The period when the two sexes were taught separately was also brief: decrease in the railroad population made the support of two teachers an extravagance, and the system died a natural death after one year: the teachers married each other and moved elsewhere. Parents remain the effective tutors of their children in manners. In turn, established emigrants serve as tutors even to adult villagers who do not grasp the fine points of life outside the village. A boy who has been studying or working away from Valdemora is an important model for his younger siblings or cousins, and his elder relations in the village look to him for a kind of expertise which they themselves lack.

These matters bring our attention once again to the characteristics of the household as the unit which possesses a unique set of outside relationships and monitors the communication between the world of the común and the world beyond the común. The essential character of the household has not changed over the years; rather, the household has come into ascendancy in more and more areas of the social life.

Marriage establishes a new legal entity, the household of man and wife. The word *casado* for married person is intimately related to *casa* (house) and reflects the emphasis placed on the establishment of a separate dwelling place for the new legal entity. In Valdemora, the ideal coincidence of marriage, establishment of independent residence, and entry into the común have already been noted, and the bachelor vecino has been seen as something of an anomaly. The male—that is, usually, the husband—is the public and official representative of the household in a variety of respects under Spanish civil law as well as in the común. His wife, however, may control as much or more property, and though she yields its administration to her husband, she maintains the power of veto over its use and disposition. As a widow, she controls part of her deceased husband's estate as well, contracts at will with her children regarding its use and disposition, and enters the civil register as a householder in her own right. Although her husband's administrative power has passed to her, it is her son who represents her on the council. (There are no known cases of resident widows without sons or sons-in-law working the land.) A widow traditionally contributed her share of flour for the cakes at San Isidro, and she represents all of her unmarried children in the burial society (though she might not attend the annual business meeting of the men). She is responsible for her household's turn in the adra, though she is automatically excused from some tasks if the community sees fit. As a widow, a woman achieves much of the status of the male vecino; as a wife, she is very nearly on an equal footing with her vecino husband. Although the husband was the usual representative for such tasks as hornero or cowherd, husbands have been known to delegate these duties to their wives, as they still delegate many business tasks under pressure of time. In contrast to the divergence of male and female spheres in public settings, men and women share equally in the management of family and household affairs, and their formal statuses in this sphere are nearly equal, though the husband is the official administrator for the joint enterprise. The near-equality of male and female statuses is closely related to the ideal of household autonomy and to the crucial importance in the social structure of the householder, male or female, married or single.

The status of householder can be achieved by single people (perhaps later in life) as well as by married couples. It is a legal status occupied either by married couples, by widowed men or women, or by single persons who have inherited estates. There is a marked tendency for people of the same generation who are qualified to be of householder status—for instance, two bachelors—to avoid residing together. Co-residence would permit only one of them, probably the elder, to hold the position of head of family. The adult woman relinquishes her own claim to this position to her husband at marriage; she may hold the position herself if she does not marry or if her husband dies.

The household is typically either the two-generation unit of a single couple and their unmarried children; a widowed person with or without unmarried children; or a single person who is of age and who holds title to lands, either because both parents are deceased or by arrangement with a widowed mother who has released title to her estate. Households composed otherwise bind atypical members by contract—as would units composed of more than one married couple or a couple and a widowed person—and these are rare. Household 1 is most atypical in this sense, supporting a collateral relation of the head in return for his herding services.[7] Household 10, two bachelor brothers, and Household 9, a widowed mother and her bachelor vecino son, are both marginal: they house remnants of nuclear families, but not more distant relations. In past times, the household often boarded hired hands, as I have said. Sometimes hired hands were relatives—extra daughters or sons of a related family—but these were bound to their employers by contract and remained legal members of their parents' households. The scarcity in the records of other forms of compound households—such as that composed of a widow and a married child—speaks for the emphasis placed on the integrity of the small unit I have described.

The "typical" household constitutes a commensal unit, a separate unit of común membership for civil and ritual purposes, and the center of a separate set of economic ties. The "atypical" or compound household contains members who are in many respects imperfectly integrated into this complex and who, sometimes, proceed from households in other villages which claim their real allegiance. The shepherd adjunct to Household 1 is a case in point. Similarly, a woman who was sent as a child to a neighboring town to be reared by her mother's relatives recalls those years as punctuated by the return to Valdemora to her own household on every occasion of ritual or familial importance. Furthermore, the adult, adjunct members of compound households yield up their decision-making powers. Any household, compound or typical, has only one legal head and one representative in the común. A widow who moves in with her married child loses her independent status: she is no longer called upon to contribute flour at San Isidro, and she is no longer a family head whose consent may be sought, for her son or son-in-law now fully takes her place. She still holds separate membership in the burial society, but she is

7. The herder, who is the family head's mother's half-brother, escapes categorization as a professional shepherd by his permanency in Valdemora and his kinship with the head, but the distance of the kinship and his outside provenience obviously enhance the marginal nature of the household.

no longer required to take part in the adra. She may still control much of an estate legally, but she is no longer mistress in her kitchen. The active vecino and his wife are the makers of decisions: the widow plays a secondary role in counseling the younger couple, and her advice is often weakened by other considerations. In Valdemora, the widowed grandmother does not have the power in her child's household which she has in her own, and she is correspondingly loath to give up her own establishment.[8]

The household is the building-block of the común; it was also the unit with reference to which towns were chartered during the repopulation. Just as the defunct pasturage league was a federation of comunes, so we may regard the común as a federation of separate households, bound by common interests and strengthened by religious ties. The sphere of común action is limited to matters of the households' common interests, be they conceived as economic, political, or religious. We have seen in chapter 6 and elsewhere that the común's focus has changed and its activities decreased in number over the period of recorded history. Differently stated, we might say that the substance of the contract between the households has changed, for the común is a group of households bound by contract to one another. Let us then return to the question of contractual relationships in the village.

A contract, formal or informal, is regarded as a necessity in binding, for whatever purpose, parties who are not sufficiently united by other ties. To contract is to admit that other ties are lacking. This admission is made with reference to virtually every party outside the nuclear family. The ideal is not to contract at all—it is to form compacts of sentiment, common interest, and love—and this is conceived to be possible only between members of the nuclear family. Thus, the ideal household of parents and unmarried children is the only unit whose members are thought to be so tightly bound by sentimental ties that no others are necessary.

8. The grandmother appears to loom larger in her child's family affairs in other parts of Spain or in other segments of society—at least this is her popular image.

When some form of compound household exists, a contracted relationship intrudes into the dwelling place and into daily relations. The only situation where contracts may be said to exist within the nuclear family household is that in which two unmarried, adult siblings live together or when an adult bachelor son, farmer or herder, is salaried by his parents for his full-time work. This is conceived, though, as beneficial to the son, or to the younger of the co-resident siblings, and we can now understand the Valdemoran's reluctance to define these people as working by contract or to discuss the nature of their salaries.

Early chapters of this book deal separately with the común organization and with a family's other alliances. But these are not totally distinct orders nor are they based on different premises. It is now possible to view the facts in perspective and to regard a household's común membership as one of its many contracted relationships.[9] The común is still unique in that it is territorially based, involves more than two parties, and has a corporate existence through time. But, as in any other contracted relationship, sentimental ties are not strong enough to maintain the común. Because its functions are crucial to its members' livelihood, the común is their most important commitment outside the family. It is significant that its functions are surrounded by ritual and by the simulation of family sentiment, for these serve to strengthen the members' bonds at the very moments when they are most threatened by household self-interest. A household's other alliances are most easily repaired or replaced: the territorial alliance cannot be broken in the traditional way of life, and while its demands might be heavy, its members are socialized to value its rewards.

The common interests which bind the households change

9. The much used *gemeinschaft-gesellschaft* distinction is not apt here either for contrasting the corporate and noncorporate aspects of social life or for describing the course of change. Such an application would simply obscure the sentimental structure common to all relationships beyond the limits of the nuclear family.

through time. Pasturage leagues are no longer of vital importance, and their very existence has been forgotten. Redistribution of meat within the común is no longer a binding interest, either, and the young are unaware that auctions ever took place or that the bids scheduled village feasts. Today, the households find that the maintenance of the sheep pastures, once a chief concern, is no longer a question of common interest or of economic necessity, and families are autonomous in deciding whether or not to herd at all. Families have been freed from cooperation in such affairs. Cooperation is viewed as a compromise necessitated by economic circumstances, damaging to household autonomy. The households could not be brought to cooperative farming as a single group, and only some found voluntary cooperation economically attractive and personally feasible. Just as pasturage leagues weakened and disappeared, it is probably accurate to describe the común as weakening through time, though sentiment clings to traditions after the economic fact.

Valdemorans hasten to agree that the most burdensome and difficult contract is with one's neighbors, for it complicates living with them in harmony. They feel that the ideal social life is that enjoyed by people who are not dependent upon one another for anything but conviviality. And yet, since the ideal settlement is dense, one should not have to go far for companionship. Thus, the ideal arrangement is again one which has been imperfectly realized in Valdemora's history: a household should be thoroughly surrounded by others (which has been true on a small scale), but it should be free to associate with others as it sees fit. The autonomy of the household in forming alliances has been achieved traditionally only in the limited social life in the networks of alliances I have outlined. On the contrary, the bulk of the household's social effort has been committed to the común in which it has compulsory membership. The ideal social life, for the Valdemoran, is attained in a large and dense settlement where within the one town or barrio he can find all the companionship he needs, where he can select his own associates, and where the people he works with are not the only available friends. This ideal is fully realized only by emigration. It is in the contrast it presents to this ideal that Valdemora most merits the designation of despoblado: it is a place with too few inhabitants to be considered a *poblado,* a peopled place, which is what a pueblo must be. The despoblado is almost an anti-pueblo because it is so small.

# Afterword

The Valdemoran concern with a sedentary way of life in a dense settlement, and the fact that this concern is apparently widespread in Spain, led me to wonder if populations which are not nucleated or not sedentary do not require study in an entirely new frame of reference. In 1968 and 1969, I worked in a geographically dispersed population of transhumant herders and found there, in old Castile but in a strikingly different setting, new versions of some of the concerns which had already become familiar.

Few points on the map of Spain can rival the Montes de Pas for their contrast to Valdemora. Most inhabitants of the province of Santander refer to their home as la Montaña and not as part of Old Castile. The inhabitants of the Montes de Pas go farther and refer to themselves only as Pasiegos, carefully delimiting their own villages from those of la Montaña. The cowherding Pasiegos, who specialize variously in dairy products and in the breeding and sale of dairy cattle, live in dispersion along montane river valleys and practice local transhumance as the pastures ripen at different altitudes. Because the fields are small, they move from one house-barn-meadow complex to another at single altitudes as well. A family may live at any of a half-dozen places during the year and, at most seasons, move as often as every two weeks. In their transhumance, the Pasiegos differ from all of the dairying villages "lower down in la Montaña," which are sedentary. Also, settlement in the Montes de Pas seems to reach an extreme of dispersion which is not duplicated in the rest of the province. Further, there is at present no trace of an indigenous corporate tradition there. The Pasiegos descend from eleventh-century cowherds who moved into the Montes de Pas with grazing rights granted by the Monastery of Oña (Burgos). Oña, and later Espinosa de los Monteros (Burgos), were the governmental centers with both civil and religious jurisdiction over the herders. The Pasiego centers did not become seats of local government until late in the seventeenth century. Most villages of Santander show much stronger corporate traditions than do the Pasiego settlements; so also do other communities of transhumant herders in Spain.

After her first trip away from the Cantabrian coast, onto the meseta, a Pasiego girl told me "how sad those Castilian pueblos are, all huddled together and everything the color of adobe." Coming from the meseta, one must adjust to the intense year-round green of the countryside, to the humid climate, to the distances between houses, and then begin to emerge points of comparison between the two extremes.

For all the dispersion and size of the municipalities, it becomes evident that the Pasiegos do not think of the large regions named on the map as being single localities. They are, rather, composed of numerous smaller, named areas, which people identify in some cases as separate "pueblos." In areas of favorable topography, habitation clusters enough that voices carry easily from one house to another. A few of these clusters achieve some embryonic religious identity with the presence of chapels. Although a family moves in and out of these centers without relation to the movements of its neighbors, a cluster at low altitude may be thought of as "home." Those who have enough rich valley meadow spend as little time as possible in the more desolate, high pastures, and for old people retirement from active herding means becoming sedentary on a single one of the family plots. People are strongly attracted by settled life in a center where there are some conveniences. I have not heard a word of praise for the nomadic existence from anyone who leads that life, and emigration has been heavy.

There is a marked change in the sexual division of labor with retirement, the adoption of sedentary life, or emigration from the pastoral community. This becomes dramatically evident in the contrast between the herding people and the commercial people of the plazas, descendants of herders, whose life style differs from that of the herders in the same respects in which the Valdemoran style differs today from that of the past. In the plazas, one even encounters some of the same mistrust of the herder that is so marked in Valdemora.

Valdemorans and Pasiegos are fleeing toward much the same thing: a settled center where one can live in comfort and not in social isolation. Here, too, the larger centers are the more attractive. In these and other respects, the extremes show us that there is a general quality in Spanish life which supersedes regional differences. The style of life in the cities is strikingly similar, though each center, of course, vigorously claims that it is the best, just as do the villages of the Sierra Ministra or the Pasiego villages and the sublocalities of each one.

But it is the differences which give texture to the whole. The Pasiego produces primarily for the market and has never been as self-sufficient as the Valdemora farmer. He adapts commercially to the city with greater ease than the Valdemoran. He is often wealthier and his progress on the social ladder is more rapid. The Valdemoran, on the other hand, is more adept at living in a community, and the closeness of his city neighbors is not strange to him. His tolerance for such closeness is great and he behaves well in it. The tensions of city life are quite different for the two kinds of emigrants: the Pasiego gains a more vigorous social life at the expense of a treasured independence, and the Valdemoran gains a desired measure of independence at the expense of his secure position in a mutual-aid society.

On the rural scene, the difference in the effects of emigration is striking. The Pasiego who has stayed in his native village has, through the emigration of many of his neighbors, achieved a larger land-base and lives in better circumstances than did his grandfather. This is also true in Valdemora. But the general outlines of Pasiego social life have not changed in kind, for the society is at base loosely knit and marked by much movement in and out of its territorial limits and up and down its social ladder. The strongest visible tradition is that of leaving individuals and families to their own affairs with minimum exercise of community constraint. There is, concomitantly, a good deal of fighting, in and out of court, and feuding. Because Valdemora has also the strong tradition of community constraint, it is vulnerable to the effects of territorial and social mobility.

The notion of family autonomy has won the day in modern Spain and is leaving in its wake the tightly corporate village traditions. Because Valdemora is not larger, richer, or in a more sought-after climate, and also because communications are good and the village has never known hunger, the pueblo has not been subject to sharp intrusions or to internal contrasts and discontent. Thus, the corporate tradition has lived on there at the will of its inhabitants. That those who have stayed show concern for their corporate future speaks for the place that the común holds in their affection. This is an affective tie of which the vecinos of few towns can boast. There is pride, even among emigrants, in their corporate history and in the traditions of social harmony which surround it. Today, the fate of the común is in the balance. The essential success of corporate life, with its frustrations and its rewards, must be measured by the fact that the común's fate lies with the vecinos themselves, who deliberate on it with care and above all with mutual respect. Huddled and adobe-colored, Valdemora does not seem sad.

# Appendix

## Archives Studied

1. Documents concerning Valdemora in the Archive of the House of Medinaceli, Casa de Pilatos, Seville

Documents are listed by their archive numbers and dates.

Medinaceli *legajo* 48–13

| | |
|---|---|
| 1539 | Accord between the House of Medinaceli and the común de vecinos of Valdemora concerning rights to the produce of the common and woodland of Valdemora |

Med. leg. 48–35

| | |
|---|---|
| 1589 | Report of election of alcalde of the mesta of the Quadrilla *(sic)* of Calzada |

Med. leg. 48–38

| | |
|---|---|
| 1650 | Report of election of alcalde of the corral of the Quadrilla of Calzada |

Med. leg. 48–43

| | |
|---|---|
| 1717 | List of member towns of the Quadrilla of Calzada; their pastures, woodlands, and other communal properties; dates of their season of open pasturage |

An unnumbered memorandum inserted between Med. leg. 48–47 and 48–48 records a (lost?) document concerning procedures for open pasturage in the towns of the Quadrilla of Calzada.

Med. leg. 48–52

1864 Record of appropriation of land for railroad construction

Med. (?) leg. 54–27

1860 Record of appropriation of land for railroad construction

2. Documents concerning Valdemora in the Archives of the Valdemora and Salcedo Parish Churches

Parish registers

1878–1900

Church accounts

1553 ff. Fragmentary at points

1820–60

Records of tithes paid to the Bishop of Sigüenza

1678–1735

1737–87

Baptismal registers

1903 A compiled index which records baptisms from 1682 to 1903

Marriage registers

1571–1679 Fragmentary at points

1851–1963

Death registers:

1895 A compiled index which records deaths from 1852 to 1858

3. Archive of the Común de Vecinos of Valdemora

Cadasters and property surveys

1760 Cadaster of the Marqués de la Ensenada, village copy; original recorded ca. 1750

1878–85

1892–93

one undated document

Section 2 excludes most of the current or more recent registers.
Section 3 excludes most of the current or more recent documents and the recent records filed in the Ayuntamiento of Aguasalida.

Auctions

| | |
|---|---|
| 1882 / 1883 / 1888 | Position of *hornero* |
| 1883–85 / 1887 / 1888 | Manure |
| 1883 | Plot of land |
| 1882 / 1883 / 1887 | Oven ashes |

Hermandad de Nuestro Señor (burial society) records, regulations, and accounts

1876
1879–1963

San Antonio pasture and feast accounts

1867
1868
1870–75
1877
1887–89

Hermandad de San Isidro fiesta accounts

1843–91
1893–98

Provision for care of draft animals by the cowherd

1866–77
1886–89
1891
1899

Provision for care of draft animals by adra

1883
1885–88
1893

Contracts with the sacristan

1868–73
1877
1882
1887

Pósito pío (communal granary) accounts

1795

1806
1813
1814
1816
1817
1819
1825–36
1854
1855
1868
1888

House inventories and accounts recorded at death of vecinos
47 documents, dated between 1780 and 1888

Miscellaneous

| | |
|---|---|
| 1857 | Record of council's empowering certain of its members to deal in its behalf with a vecino of Sigüenza |
| 1857 | Record of donation by four vecinos of 4000 *reales de vellón* and 72 fanegas of wheat to the town in time of need; conditions for their reimbursement |
| 1865 | Contract with a doctor for services |
| 1866 | Description of the boundaries between Salcedo, Valdemora, and Molinos |
| 1869 | Accounts of three vecinos for services rendered to the town |
| 1882, 1888 | Records of the fixing of irrigation turns; one undated document included |
| 1883, 1884 | Contract with a schoolteacher |
| 1888 | Request to the railroad for the use of certain resources near the tracks |
| 1890 | Regulations for celebration of San Roque fiesta |
| 1907 | Contract with a doctor for services |
| 1911 | Description of the boundaries between Valdemora, Salcedo, Molinos, Aguasalida, and Mazarulleque established in 1801 |
| 1923 | Provision for cession of land and labor for extension of the cemetery; regulations governing the use of cemetery plots |

# Glossary

Spanish terms which recur in the text are listed here with their local meanings, which may or may not correspond with one of the meanings given for the term (if it is recognized) in the *Diccionario de la lengua española* (Real Academia Española 1956). Words set in SMALL CAPS are defined elsewhere in the glossary.

ABAJO, DE
: From below; refers to the people of the railroad settlement.

ADRA
: The rotation of responsibilities on the basis of house order in the pueblo.

ALCALDE
: Mayor, or president of the AYUNTAMIENTO. The *alcalde pedáneo* is the mayor of a dependent hamlet. The *alcalde* of the MESTA or of the *corral* were the officials of the defunct town league for pasturage.

ALDEA
: Hamlet, or small settlement, usually dependent upon a larger seat of government.

ALGUACIL
: Aide, an AYUNTAMIENTO official.

ALJAMA
: Jewish population or sector of a town in the Middle Ages.

ARROBA
: Measures now largely obsolete, equivalent to 11.5 kg. solid or 16 liters liquid.

**Ayuntamiento**
: Municipal government.

**Boina**
: Beret.

**Camino de Santiago**
: Road to Santiago (de Compostela), Galicia; medieval pilgrimage route.

**Campo**
: Countryside; the uninhabited areas of the municipality.

**Casado (casada)**
: Married man or woman.

**Celemín**
: One-twelfth of the Castilian fanega of surface or volume, now largely obsolete. The celemín of wheat is equivalent to about 3.66 kg.

**Cendera**
: Communal labor on public property.

**Cocido**
: Stew with legume base, usually chick-peas in Castile.

**Común de vecinos**
: The village corporation consisting of the nuclear families of active or retired farmers.

**Concejo**
: The executive body of the común de vecinos consisting of the heads of farm families.

**Cuadrilla**
: Town league for joint pasturage, now defunct. *Cuadrilla de Calzada* was the league of which Valdemora was a member. In the *Hermandad del Cabildo* a *cuadrilla* is a group of ten lambs.

**Derrota**
: The entrance of livestock into recently harvested fields to graze grain stubble.

**Despoblado**
: A very small settlement.

**Fanega**
: The *fanega* of volume is the amount of grain required to sow one *fanega* (surface) of land. The Castilian *fanega* of land is 2236 square meters, i.e., 0.2236 hectares. The *fanega* of wheat is 43.5 kg., of barley 37.0 kg., and of oats 27.0 kg.

**Fincas perdidas**
: Lost or waste fields; low quality fields once sown but now permanently fallow.

Forastero (forastera)
A person from any other municipality; most often applied to males.

Fuero
Royal grant of the Middle Ages delimiting area and conditions of jurisdiction of either persons or population centers. *Fuero* may refer to the territorial entity as well as to the documents of charter.

Gachas (de miel)
A type of porridge, in this case made of wheat flour and sweetened with honey.

Gananciales
Earned or acquired, as opposed to inherited, wealth or property.

Hermandad
Brotherhood or confraternity. *Hermandad del Cabildo* is the Brotherhood of the Council House, the organization centered in Salcedo which levies lambs as entrance fees. *Hermandad de San Isidro* is the Brotherhood of San Isidro, the patron saint of Valdemora. *Hermandad de Nuestro Señor* is the Valdemora burial society.

Hermano (Hermana)
Member of the *Hermandad de Nuestro Señor*, the burial society of Valdemora.

Hijo (hija) del pueblo
Child of a común family.

Hornacha
Straw-burning wall oven used mostly in summer.

Hornero
Custodian of the communal oven.

Hilandera
Term applied in some regions to spinning or sewing gatherings of women and girls.

Jueves Lardero
"Fat Thursday"; Carnival Thursday.

Lavadero
Communal laundry place.

Marca mediana
The "Central Frontier" of the peninsula under the Caliphate of Córdoba, with military headquarters first at Toledo and later at Medinaceli.

Mayordomo
: Official of an HERMANDAD or brotherhood. These are sometimes called *piostres* in Valdemora's burial society.

Mejora
: Testamentary accretion of the portion of an estate destined for a given heir.

Merienda
: Elaborate afternoon snack which may reach feast proportions.

Mesta
: Organization of herders, either local or national. The *Honrado Concejo de la Mesta* was the Royal Mesta.

Mozo (moza)
: Young man or woman who has passed his or her seventeenth birthday but is unmarried.

Mudéjares
: Moslems under Christian domain in medieval Spain.

Mujer
: Woman; wife. *Las mujeres* are the común wives.

Niño (niña)
: Girl or boy, no longer a baby *(crío)*, but below age seventeen.

Novio (novia)
: Fiancé(e); terms also applied to bride and groom. Although often loosely translated as "boy [or girl] friend," the term implies marital intentions or formal engagement. *Novio* FORASTERO is a fiancé or boyfriend from another village.

Noviazgo
: Formal engagement to be married.

Padrinos
: Godparents; *padrino* means godfather, *madrina* means godmother. Godparenthood is contracted for weddings, baptisms, and confirmations.

Paseo
: Promenade, afternoon stroll.

Peseta
: Modern Spanish currency. One U.S. dollar presently equals 70 *pesetas,* but was equivalent to 60 *pesetas* at the time of the field research.

Pósito pío
: Communal granary, now defunct.

Prado
: Common meadow where draft animals were pastured.

Real

Formerly a coin. The *real de vellón* was of an alloy of silver and copper. Its equivalence in *maravedis* varied. Older people today still speak of the *real*—its modern equivalent is 0.25 pesetas.

RENFE

Red Nacional de los Ferrocarriles Españoles, Spanish National Railways.

Rollo

Ring-shaped cake made for fiestas, today associated most specifically with the fiesta of San Isidro.

Sopeta

Fiesta food of bread soaked in sweetened red wine.

Sorteo

Drawing of lots.

Sortía

Rotation on the basis of plot order—for example, for irrigation turns—now obsolete.

Teniente alcalde

Vice-alcalde.

Tercero

Third; an ayuntamiento official.

Tío (tía)

Terms for "uncle" and "aunt" which are extended also to certain categories of non-kin.

Trillo

Tribulum; flint-toothed threshing sledge.

Vaquero

Cowherd.

Vecino

Literally, "neighbor"; household head and member of the común de vecinos.

Villa

Population center with special privileges, usually seigniorial, which distinguishes it from other towns and hamlets.

# References

Publications of the Consejo Superior de Investigaciones Científicas are designated by the abbreviation CSIC.

Amador de los Ríos, J.
1960 Historia social, política, y religiosa de los judíos de España y Portugal. Madrid, Aguilar.

Ateneo Científico, Literario y Artístico de Madrid
1901 Información promovida por la sección de ciencias morales y políticas en el curso de 1901 a 1902, circular y cuestionario. (Village responses were filed in 1966 in Museo Nacional de Etnología, Madrid.)

Barnes, J. A.
1954 Class and committees in a Norwegian island parish. Human Relations 7:39–58.

Cagigas, I. de las
1947 Minorías étnico-religiosas de la Edad Media española. Vol. 1, Los Mozárabes. Madrid, CSIC.

Campbell, J. K.
1964 Honour, family and patronage: a study of institutions and moral values in a Greek mountain community. Oxford, Clarendon Press.

Cantera Burgos, F.
1955 Sinagogas españolas. Madrid, CSIC.

Caro Baroja, J.
1957 El sociocentrismo de los pueblos españoles. *In* Razas, pueblos y linajes. Madrid, Revista de Occidente.

1961 Los judíos en la España moderna y contemporánea. Madrid, Ediciones Arion.

Castro, A.
1954 The structure of Spanish history. Princeton, Princeton University Press.

Código civil español, legislaciones forales o especiales y leyes complementarias.
1966 Madrid, Instituto Editorial Reus.

Costa, J.
1898 Colectivismo agrario en España. Madrid.
1902 Derecho consuetudinario y economía popular de España. Vol. 1, Alto Aragón. Barcelona, Manuel Soler.

Costa, J., et al.
1902 Derecho consuetudinario y economía popular de España. Vol. 2. Barcelona, Manuel Soler.

Dias, A. J.
1948 Vilarinho da Furna, uma aldeia comunitária. Porto, Instituto de Alta Cultura.
1953 Rio de Onor, comunitarismo agro-pastoril. Porto, Instituto de Alta Cultura.

Fél, E., and Hofer, T.
1969 Proper peasants: traditional life in a Hungarian village. Viking Fund Publications in Anthropology no. 46. New York, Wenner-Gren Foundation for Anthropological Research.

Fernández de Béthencourt, F.
1904 Medinaceli. Historia genealógica y heráldica de la monarquía española. Vol. 5. Madrid.

Foster, G. M.
1960 Culture and conquest: America's Spanish heritage. Viking Fund Publications in Anthropology no. 27. New York, Wenner-Gren Foundation for Anthropological Research.
1961 The dyadic contract: a model for the social structure of a Mexican peasant village. American Anthropologist 63:1173–92.
1963 The dyadic contract in Tzintzuntzan, II: patron-client relationship. American Anthropologist 65:1280–94.

Freeman, S. T.
1968a Corporate village organisation in the Sierra Ministra: an Iberian structural type. Man (n.s.) 3:477–84.

1968b Religious aspects of the social organization of a Castilian village. American Anthropologist 70:34–49.

Friedl, E.
1964 Vasilika, a village in modern Greece. New York, Holt, Rinehart and Winston.

García-Badell, G.
1963 Introducción a la historia de la agricultura española. Madrid, CSIC.

Gearing, F. O.
1967 *Review of* J. G. Peristiany, ed., Honour and shame: the values of Mediterranean society. American Anthropologist 69:520–22.

Geertz, C.
1960 The Javanese *kijaji:* the changing role of a cultural broker. Comparative Studies in Society and History 2:228–49.

Gluckman, M.
1963 Gossip and scandal. Current Anthropology 4:307–16.

González, J.
1951 Reconquista y repoblación de Castilla, León, Extremadura y Andalucía (siglos XI a XIII). *In* La reconquista española y la repoblación del país. Zaragoza, CSIC.
1960 El reino de Castilla en la época de Alfonso VIII. Madrid, CSIC.

Homans, G. C.
1941 English villagers of the thirteenth century. Cambridge, Mass., Harvard University Press.

Instituto Nacional de Estadística
1960 Censo de la población y de las viviendas de España. Madrid.

Jimeno, E.
1958 Transformaciones en el mapa de Soria (1594–1833). Celtiberia 8:213–31.

Kenny, M.
1960 Patterns of patronage in Spain. Anthropological Quarterly 33:14–23.
1962 A Spanish tapestry: town and country in Castile. Bloomington, Indiana University Press.

Klein, J.
1920 The Mesta: a study in Spanish economic history, 1273–1836. Cambridge, Mass., Harvard University Press.

Layna Serrano, F.
1948 La provincia de Guadalajara. Madrid, Hauser y Menet.
1960 Castillos de Guadalajara. Madrid.
Lévi-Provençal, E.
1957 España musulmana hasta la caida del califato de Córdoba, 711–1031, instituciones y arte. Madrid, Espasa-Calpe.
Levy, H.
1956 Property distribution by lot in present-day Greece. Transactions of the American Philological Association 87:42–46.
Lisón-Tolosana, C.
1966 Belmonte de los Caballeros: a sociological study of a Spanish town. Oxford, Clarendon Press.
López Morán, E.
1902 León. *In* J. Costa, et al.
Madoz, P.
1849 Diccionario geográfico-estadístico-histórico de España y sus posesiones de ultramar. Madrid.
Minguella y Arnedo, T.
1910 Historia de la diócesis de Sigüenza y de sus obispos. Madrid.
Nuevo atlas de España
1961 Madrid, Aguilar.
Paine, R.
1967 What is gossip about? An alternative hypothesis. Man (n.s.) 2:278–85.
Paz y Melia, A.
1922 Documentos del archivo y biblioteca del Exmo. Señor Duque de Medinaceli. Madrid.
Peristiany, J. G., ed.
1966 Honour and shame: the values of Mediterranean society. Chicago, University of Chicago Press.
Pitt-Rivers, J. A.
1958 Ritual kinship in Spain. Transactions of the New York Academy of Sciences (Series 2) 20:424–31.
1961 The people of the sierra. Chicago, University of Chicago Press.
Rabal, N.
1889 Soria. *In* España: sus monumentos y artes, su naturaleza e historia. Barcelona.

Real Academia Española
1956 Diccionario de la lengua española (18th edition). Madrid, Espasa-Calpe.
Regatillo, E. F.
1965 Derecho parroquial. Santander, Editorial Sal Terrae.
Reyes, A.
1960 Introductory note to Poema del Cid. Mexico, Espasa-Calpe Mexicana.
Roth, C.
1947 A history of the Marranos. Philadelphia, Jewish Publication Society of America.
Sanders, I. T.
1949 Balkan village. Lexington, University of Kentucky Press.
Serrano Gómez, J.
1902 Burgos, Soria, Logroño. *In* J. Costa et al.
Silverman, S. F.
1965 Patronage and community-nation relationships in central Italy. Ethnology 4:172–89.
Smith, W. R.
1914 Lectures on the religion of the Semites. London, Adam and Charles Black.
Taracena, B., and Tudela, J.
1962 Guía de Soria y su provincia. Madrid, Revista de Occidente.
Thomas, H.
1961 The Spanish civil war. New York, Harper and Row.
Tudela, J.
1949 Notas de geografía social: las migraciones profesionales sorianas. *In* Homenaje a Don Luis de Hoyos Sainz 2:391–400. Madrid.
Unamuno, M. de
1902 Vizcaya. *In* J. Costa, et al.
Valdeavellano, L. G. de
1968 Curso de historia de las instituciones españolas de los orígenes al final de la Edad Media. Madrid, Revista de Occidente.
Wolf, E. R.
1956 Aspects of group relations in a complex society: Mexico. American Anthropologist 58:1056–78.

# Index

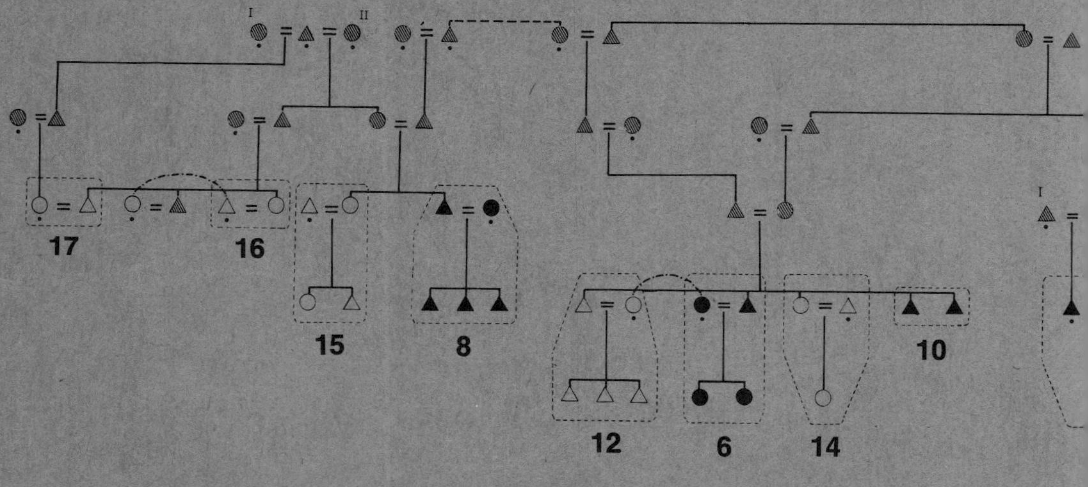

I
II
17
16
15
8
12
6
14
10
I